THE MASEYTOYS GUIDE TO MATCHBOX

NEIL MASEY

*Matchbox® and associated trade marks and trade dress
are owned by and used licence from Mattel Inc.©Mattel Inc. 2022.
All rights reserved.
Mattel makes no representation as to the authenticity
of the materials contained herein.
All opinions are those of the author and not of Mattel.*

*All Matchbox® images and art are owned by Mattel Inc.
©2022 Mattel Inc. All rights reserved.*

All rights reserved
Copyright © Neil Masey, 2022

The right of Neil Masey to be identified as the author
of thiswork has been asserted in accordance with Section 78
of the Copyright, Designs and Patents Act 1988

The book cover is copyright to Neil Masey

This book is published by
Grosvenor House Publishing Ltd
Link House
140 The Broadway, Tolworth, Surrey, KT6 7HT.
www.grosvenorhousepublishing.co.uk

This book is sold subject to the conditions that it shall not, by way of
trade or otherwise, be lent, resold, hired out or otherwise circulated
without the author's or publisher's prior consent in any form of binding
or cover other than that in which it is published and
without a similar condition including this condition being imposed
on the subsequent purchaser.

A CIP record for this book
is available from the British Library

ISBN: 978-1-80381-340-0

*For my Dad, Donald Masey
and for my late Mum, Olive Masey.
Between them they passed
the collecting bug onto me.*

*Also, for that bloke
who bought my toy collection
for a song in 1981.
It planted the seed
for Maseytoys to flourish.*

Grosvenor House Publishing

CHAPTERS

INTRODUCTION	3
HACKNEY INDUSTRIAL HISTORY	15
THE BIRTH OF LESNEY PRODUCTS	17
A THIRD PARTNER	23
BEGINNING THE 1-75 RANGE – A NEW ERA	35
GLOBAL EXPANSION	55
THE WORKFORCE	73
WORKFORCE RELATIONS AND CONDITIONS	81
A CHALLENGER THE PERFECT STORM	93
HOT WHEELS IMPACT	105
THE DREADED 1970's AND 1980's	115
GUIDE NOTES	125
MATCHBOX PRICE GUIDE	129

INTRODUCTION

THE FIRST DIECAST TOY I ever saw was a Dinky No. 151 Triumph 1800 in tan with green hubs. It was around 1969, and as a small child of six I had sneaked up into the loft and found my older brother's toy collection. He had been given various toy cars by my gran in the 1950s, and to me it was fascinating to see this ancient, dusty treasure from a bygone age. I was intrigued, and I wanted to find out more.

I was happy to play with these and other toy cars, but I was never interested in smashing them up or destroying them in any way. My passion was collecting toy cars that were old and obsolete, no longer produced, no longer played with or loved, and when I found the rest of my brother's small collection, I cleaned each toy up before proudly displaying them in my bedroom.

My late mother was an avid jumble sale-goer, and she loved a bargain, so we would go to jumble sales every Saturday and I would always pick up toy cars which had invariably been manufactured the decade before, in the 1950s. We were a small family, living on a newly created local authority housing estate, and we mainly played with second-hand toys rather than brand new, and it was usual for us to be given hand-me-downs or toys from jumble sales. I have a long-lasting and distinct memory of seeing the bonnet and grille of a Matchbox Trojan Van poking up out of the tarmac in the road outside our house. My dad told me that in 1960 the road had been resurfaced, and some poor child's toy had obviously been left out in the road and subsequently got frozen in time by the molten black Tarmac laid by the workmen. My instant reaction was that I wanted to dig it out and preserve it in some way, although I never did of course. That Matchbox toy was always there in the road for as long as I can remember, with its surface getting more and more worn away and shiny each day as it was driven over, until around 1980 when the road was resurfaced again, and it was gone forever.

My particular interest in Matchbox came soon after I first discovered my brother's collection. I bought a No.17 Removal Van at a jumble sale, followed by the No.50 Pick Up and some other models from a trip to junk shops with my dad. At that time in the late 1960s, our local toy shops would heavily reduce the price of Matchbox toys when new models were announced, so that they could free up more shelf space for the new arrivals. Learning the art of bargain hunting from my mother, I managed to get quite a few gems, which I took home and admired before displaying them in my room. They were never heavily played with, just admired and closely studied before being put on show in my bedroom.

Soon, with the advent of pocket money, paper rounds, milk rounds, and lots of car washing, I had my own money to be able to shop for the toys I wanted. I did stray from Matchbox a little, having bought a beautiful Corgi Heinkel from the Ridgeway Stores in Chobham, Surrey, and many, many Dinkys from Ashplants toy shop in Woking, which were all at heavily reduced in prices. They were almost all obsolete and discontinued models (hence the prices), and that's exactly what I loved collecting until the Superfast era came about.

Unlike most 'normal' children, I didn't stop playing with toy cars ever! I had accumulated enough toys when I was an early teenager for my mum to buy me a mahogany, glass-fronted display cabinet which she got as a second-hand bargain (obviously!) for £10. In this cabinet I carefully placed my polished, treasured, and pristine toy collection, along with a pocket book from WH Smiths where I had written down all the toys that I had collected. I continued collecting right up until I was 18, and then in 1981 my interest waned when I discovered drinking, nightclubs, and bars.

I cannot now remember exactly what drove the decision I was about to make about my toy collection. Maybe my mind had been addled by drinking and dancing, or maybe I was looking to buy my first full-sized real car. My beloved mother would have been able to tell me exactly what was behind it, but sadly she died in 1993, so I have no clue as to why I did what I did. But in 1981, I advertised my toy collection for sale.

The Surrey Advertiser was a local, county-wide newspaper which carried a free advertising section, and this is where I placed my ad. Rather than actually paying for an advert, I followed my mother's instinct of a bargain! Soon enough, we got a phone call from a man who was interested in buying them. He had travelled to our house in Woking from Kingston or Surbiton, which at the time I thought was quite a long way to come and view my toys. The man spent what seemed like hours studying each of my models before making me an offer. Not having yet honed my negotiating skills, I readily accepted the £1000 cash he offered me for them. He then gathered them all up, loaded them in his van, along with the mahogany cabinet, and away he went. All I was left with was my WH Smith notebook with the model numbers I had lovingly collected since the age of six.

What became of the money is lost in time. I certainly didn't buy a car until 1984, choosing instead to buy a new stereo: a top-of--range Sharp VZ3510 system, which played vinyl records vertically and which incorporated a tape deck and stereo radio. Other than that, I am fairly sure the money was frittered away at the weekends amongst the nightclubs of Kingston, Guildford, and Camberley. And with that, the 12-year legacy of my collecting had gone, washed away in a few weekends with the help of many glasses of Pernod and Blackcurrant (my preferred tipple at the age of 18).

I bought a car eventually, and moved out of the family home and into an apartment in Guildford, after which I embarked upon a successful career in mortgage lending and sought my pleasures in other ways. Occasionally, though, I would look at my list of toys and wonder where they were now and why I had sold them in the first place.Fast forward 20 years to 2001. I was then 38 years of age and, during a house move, I found my notebook with the list of toys I had lovingly collected from 1969 to 1981. It made me incredibly sad to see that list, written in my juvenile hand and detailing everything I had collected, the condition of each model, and the estimated value of them at the time. I had clearly loved them and enjoyed collecting them, so why did I make the decision to sell? I worked out that £1000 in 1981 was equivalent to about £3000 in 2001, and I wondered what £3000 would buy me now by way of Matchbox toys, but it wasn't very many at all. Then I set about cross-referencing every Matchbox toy I had listed with a model toys' price guide to see how easy it would be to re-collect everything. When I had finished, I had calculated that I needed something in the region of £10,000 in order to re-collect all those treasured models which I had sold for a song. I didn't have £10,000 at the time, and I was feeling quite down about it, so I hatched a plan which would start me on a path of mammoth buying and selling.

In 2001 I decided that the only way I could start collecting again was to invest in job lots of Matchbox toys at auction, keep the ones that I wanted in order to restore my collection, and sell the rest. The hope was that I would make some money back in the process, too. It was a simple plan, and it signalled the beginning of maseytoys – a business which I have run ever since, buying and selling Matchbox toys at many different events, including toy fairs, via magazines, online, and on eBay. The business has gone from strength to strength, and in 2021 it recorded its highest ever sales. Maseytoys has sold over 100,000 models since 2001, and thankfully I have managed to retain a few gems to add to my collection. Over the years I have sold almost every variant that Matchbox produced, except for those rarities and pre-production models which have sold at auction for many thousands of pounds. I still absolutely adore the models, and I am enthralled by the business created by two fascinating men, the history, the growth of the business, the stories of the factories and facilities Lesney built, and the loyalty of the staff (just one strike in their 30-year history!).

I visited the last Lesney building across the bridge from the Lea Conservatory Road, Hackney, London complex, before it was bulldozed to make way for the Olympic Stadium. The building had housed the administration offices, wages department, and car parts division, and I was very fortunate to be granted permission to go into the building. I photographed the dishevelled interior, the disused production line area, the canteen, and various communal areas, and I wondered what it would have been like to work there, amongst the c.4000 strong workforce. After negotiation, I was allowed to take away some of the fixings (clocking-in machine, production signage, etc), which I still have today. I also negotiated with the selling agents on the famous Perspex Lesney Products & Co. Ltd. sign which topped the building, but in the end it was agreed by all that this should be donated to the Hackney Museum, which is its rightful home.

In 2016 I decided to write this book, which was eventually completed in late 2018. It goes without saying that I was incredulous to find that I had somehow mislaid the memory drive on which the manuscript was stored. I searched everywhere for it, and after many months there was nothing else I could do but to re-write the whole thing all over again! After I finished the second edition a year later, I found the missing drive when I was clearing out my van before selling it; it had fallen into a crevice in the cab, presumably from my pocket.

I plan to update the book each year with guide prices for each model, and to periodically produce more books about the other ranges Lesney produced. I do not plan, however, to have to write any of these books twice!

No.1a Aveling Barford Road Roller

Note the hand painted trim!

No.1a Aveling Barford Road Roller

Straight (most common) roof type

No.1b Aveling Barford Road Roller

No.2a Muir Hill Dumper

With harder to find green diecast wheels

MATCHBOX HISTORY

HACKNEY INDUSTRIAL HISTORY

IN THE EARLY 1800s, the area of Hackney in north London was a rural community consisting mostly of pasture and market gardens. In 1790, Lewes Berger started the beginnings of his paint manufacturing empire which, by the mid-1800s, employed upwards of 500 people in Hackney. The industrial revolution really took hold in Hackney at this time, mainly due to the location of the river, which was used to transport goods and as a dumping ground for noxious waste. During this era there were three other main industries present – rope making, porcelain production and optical glass making – and in 1862 the first plastics were manufactured in the UK by Alexander Parkes in Wallis Road.

By the early 20th century the biggest employer was the confectioner and jam maker Clarke, Nickolls, and Coombes, which later became Trebor Sharps. Ahead of their time, they introduced profit sharing for their employees and convalescent homes for their retired workers, which may have been an inspiration for

Lesney's excellent benefits scheme. By far the biggest industry in Hackney in the early 1900s was footwear and clothing, which employed upwards of 20,000 people around 1920, and spawned famous names such as Daks and Moss Bros. And other firms introduced yet more benefits for staff, such as sports facilities and bath houses.

Before the Second World War Hackney had over 2,000 factories, and it had long been established as a centre for industry. After the war, London's industries decentralised and firms moved away, with only a few of the larger industries remaining, such as rubber making and chemical manufacturing. When the Lesney business was established in 1947, the area was a mixture of small industries, a couple of large manufacturing units, and many bomb-damaged buildings.

There is a tenuous link with Lesney and the city bankers C. Hoare & Company. The bank was established in 1672 by Henry Hoare, and around 1800 they bought the Red Lion Brewery in East Smithfield, and the brewer Hoare & Co. was established. Although the brewery was later swallowed up by the enormous Charrington Brewery, the banking firm still survives in London today and it is still run by the descendants of Henry Hoare.

THE BIRTH OF LESNEY PRODUCTS

AT THE END OF A DARK ALLEY at the northern boundary of Tottenham stood the Rifleman public house – a pub owned by Hoare & Co. Having suffered considerable bomb damage, it had been abandoned and was now in a bit of a sorry state; the broken reeded glass windows had been used as targets for local boys throwing stones, the bar had been removed and chopped for firewood, and the pumps no longer assisted the flow of amber nectar. But it was available to let for the very reasonable rent of £2 and 10 shillings a week, and it was in the perfect location for what it was to become.

Leslie Smith and his friend Rodney Smith had both served in the Second World War, Leslie in the Royal Navy and Rodney in the Royal Engineers. Lesley saw action at the D Day Landings, and they had both fought in the Dieppe raid in 1942. The two men had built a good friendship over the years, deciding to remain in touch and perhaps even work together one day after the war.

Leslie's father owned a building firm, and at 27 years of age he was juggling working in his father's firm alongside employment as a carpet export buyer. Rodney was working for the local firm Die Cast Machine Tools (DCMT), and soon the conversations turned to the experience he was gaining working for a firm whose diecast components were in very high demand.

As was the custom at the time, ex-servicemen received a gratuity to assist them after the war. Rodney received £90 and Leslie had £200; with this and a further sum of £210, they accumulated a total of £500 to start their business. They paid the rental deposit and took over the dilapidated pub, and Rodney installed in the basement a hand-operated diecast machine bought for a song from DCMT. The ground floor was to be used for assembly, and the first floor for offices and storage, once the floor had been strengthened (presumably by Leslie's builder dad).

It was on 19th January, 1947, that their tiny diecasting business, Lesney Products & Co. Ltd was established in the run-down, bomb-damaged pub.

Lesney Foundrey Worker

With all the machinery, the compressor and the diecasting machine, it was a noisy, dirty, and busy business. John Kendall, who was an early employee, described how there were two pots of molten metal kept on a gas flame, and he used to transfer the liquid metal from the larger pot to the smaller one, ready for filling the dies. As it was a stifling, hot, and dirty environment, the windows were open all year long for ventilation, and most of the engineers just wore vests and trousers or shorts, even in the bitter winters of post-war England.

> **From designing a model to full production took between 12 and 18 months**

Lesney began making ceiling hooks for industry and car components for the motor trade, and the business soon became established in these fields of work. Don Rix worked as a toolmaker for Lesney, and he too had seen action in the Second World War. At Normandy, he had taken a Luger gun from a fallen German soldier, which he kept loaded at the pub to ward off potential thieves.

Using this gun, he made a replica toy gun which got them all thinking about how to keep the business running between contracts for industrial parts. Perhaps they should start making toys as well as industrial parts?

No.3a Cement Mixer

Early version showing the rear handle

No.4a Massey Harris Tractor

Mudguards were ommited on the later 4a

No.4b Massey Harris Tractor

No.5a London Bus

First series bright yellow labels

No.5b London Bus

Featured a more detailed grille

No.5b London Bus

With Player's decals and grey plastic wheels

A THIRD PARTNER

JOHN (JACK) ODELL WAS BORN IN MARCH 1920 into a working-class family in London, where he was raised at 1 Wetherill Road, Muswell Hill, with his brother Ken. He had been expelled from school as a boy and had variously been described as a maverick, perfectionist, bloody minded, and a rule breaker. He certainly enjoyed a diverse spread of jobs before the war, such as van driving, estate agency, cinema projectionist, and die casting engineer.

It was the skills and tenacity he learned in these jobs and during the Second World War that he would later put to good use in setting Lesney products onto a stellar path to success.

Leslie Smith and Jack Odell

Jack initially joined the Royal Army Service Corps at the outbreak of the war, then joined the Royal Electrical

Mechanical Engineers (REME), which incidentally my own father joined around 1954, having left the Coldstream Guards some years before. REME gave Jack a trade as a mechanic and he served them for five years, seeing action with the 8th Army in North Africa, achieving the rank of sergeant and overseeing the repair and maintenance of many types of military vehicles.

> Jack Odell's army radio call sign during WWII was 'lledo'

Whilst serving in Cairo and Alexandria, ever the entrepreneur, Jack happened upon a small but lucrative business, where he would buy spares for Primus stoves and establish himself as a stove repairman. He was evidently very good at this, and he accumulated quite a good sum, around £300, which was enough to pay for his marriage shortly after the war.

In civvy street, Jack first started work for the then small diecasting company, Diecast Machine Tools (DCMT) in North London, where he worked alongside Rodney Smith. He was initially employed to sweep the floors for 3 shillings and 6 pence a week, but clearly this wasn't the job for an aspiring entrepreneur, and he eventually got work in the company's tool room.

During his time at DCMT, he thought of several ways

to establish himself in business, and he saved up enough money to buy his own moulds then began to make his own casts. He decided to set up his diecasting business from home, and he managed to buy six ex-military die-casting machines in Luton, Bedfordshire, for £60. He planned on setting up his business operating these machines in his mother's garage, but was refused permission by the local council who would not allow industrial works to be established from a residential property. The little start-up business had hit the buffers! In the winter of 1947, Leslie Smith was still in a salaried employment whilst Rodney Smith was on his own at the bombed-out pub, getting things established, when Jack popped by. Jack and Rodney got chatting about their time at DCMT and how they had both decided there was room for more diecasting firms in north London. Jack saw the opportunity that faced him: he had six diecasting machines and nowhere to operate them from. So it was agreed that he would install them in the pub and work from there. For a while, the two businesses operated in the same building. Jack had an initial order for a few thousand diecast string cutters, but he made various diecast items including, it is reported, jewellery. Before the Second World War, the UK toy distribution firm J Kohnstam (Moko) was importing Jumbo the Elephant, a large tinplate toy, from Blomer and Schuler in Germany. Lesney already had a business relationship with Kohnstam, and in particular Julius Kohnstam, who was managing the firm at that time. He suggested that Lesney make a copy of it, where the originally designed diecast legs could easily be swapped for tinplate should the upcoming zinc embargo hit the business.

Lesney were never particularly happy to make the toy, as they were essentially diecasters and not tinplate manufacturers, however they did produce quite a few of them which very occasionally come up for auction today (the early blue boxed versions had no mention of Moko on them, and it is these which are highly sought after).

During downtimes between contracts, the business struggled, and whilst searching for the next contract the firm was contacted by a local business, M.Y. Dart, who manufactured dart boards and other toys. M.Y. Dart enquired if Lesney could make a part for their handcuffs, and if they could manufacture a diecast cap gun, the BCM Space Outlaw.

Lesney agreed the contract for this, and in doing so it broadened the company output which, up until now, had concentrated mainly on electrical fittings and components. This got the Lesney partners thinking much more seriously about producing toys, and with this in mind they purchased a few Dinky toys to assess the viability of the project.

They eventually made a copy of the Road Roller, Cement Mixer, and Bulldozer, which they, crucially, sold for about a third of the price of the Dinky version. Dinky were very sniffy about who could be a stockist of their products and who could not, but Lesney stole a march on them as they would sell to any business who would accept them. They went about touting these toys, along with Jumbo the Elephant, to local shops and wholesalers in Tottenham, north London. Whilst some of the shops dismissed the wannabe Dinky toys as Christmas cracker trash, they did start to sell quite a few locally, and this eventually caught the eye of Woolworths.

Woolworths was one of those 'lower end' retailers that Dinky did not want to see selling their toys. But the canny buyers at Woolworths saw the advantage of what Lesney were offering: a Dinky-type toy at a third of the price, which was right up their street! Soon enough,

> **The original brass Road Roller prototype cost £5 to make. It went on to sell in 100s of thousands!**

Woolworths were putting in large enough orders for these toys to be distributed nationally into their stores. The business flourished until the outbreak of the Korean War in 1950, when things took a turn for the worst. The UK government then imposed restrictions on the use of zinc in non-essential products, as it was needed to make armaments, and these restrictions remained in place for two years.

During this time, Rodney Smith, seeing a decline in profits, decided to leave the company. Rodney lived on a farm and had a half share in a boat-yard, so he wanted to explore his passions (which also included the delivery of luxury yachts) and to scope out the possibility of buying a smallholding. He sold his share of the business for £8,000, which was a very tidy sum – equivalent to around £250,000 today.

In 1969 Leslie Smith bought Poole Harbour Yacht Club, his son John Smith has been the chairman since 1972 and his grandson Nick Smith is the Managing Director – it is now known as Salterns Marina.

But by 1954, Rodney was back diecasting again, after Lesney had given him much of their old manufacturing plant, and he was now making copies of their earlier models. He joined Morris and Stone in Hackney, London, to produce their Morestone and Budgie ranges, using the skills gained at Lesney to produce their Esso Petrol Pump series, which would have been a direct competitor to the Lesney range. Whilst this must have been quite difficult for Lesley Smith to deal with, it was relatively short-lived, as Rodney soon left Morestone and eventually went to live in Australia. During this troubled period, the only product to leave the Lesney factory was Jumbo, the hollow tinplate clockwork elephant.

When Rodney Smith left the company, it must have been a natural progression for Jack to abandon his business and join Lesney. After all, they had lost a diecast engineer in Rodney, and Jack had all the skills needed to replace him.

For a while the firm produced a small range of larger scale diecast toys alongside their main products, which included the Road Roller, Cement Mixer, Horse Drawn Milk Cart, Rag and Bone Cart, Caterpillar Crawler and Bulldozer, Site Dumper, Prime Mover, Massey Harris Tractor, and Covered Wagon. They also produced a diecast bait press and a Muffin The Mule stringed puppet from the UK TV series.

The bait press achieves good values today, despite it not being a toy. However, Muffin the Mule is much more sought after. In fact, all these early models fetch very high values today. For example, I sold a tiny, sugar cube-sized, diecast crate, which was one of the accessories for the Rag and Bone cart, for a staggering £39 in 2018!

Initially, these larger scale products were sold to small London toy stores, before Lesney approached larger companies and ultimately achieved nationwide distribution. But it was in 1953 that the seeds of their enormous success were established, in the making of the replica Coronation Coach. The coach had originally been produced around three years earlier for the Festival of Britain, but production had been halted when the zinc embargo came into force.

> **In 1952, 300 large scale Coronation Coaches were made in error: they had the recently departed King still in them. The Coronation would feature just one person in the carriage – the Queen.**

When King George died in 1952, the coronation of the new Queen Elizabeth was excitingly anticipated by a hugely patriotic and royalist nation, so it was inevitable that the Coronation Coach would be brought back into production.

Interestingly, the original coach had been produced with

two figures inside (the King and Queen), but after a few hundred of the re-issued models had been produced, they realised that the new Queen would be sitting in the carriage on her own during the procession, without anyone by her side. So the tooling was altered to remove the King, albeit only from the legs up, as the legs remained in the coach casting (look out for Coronation Coaches with TWO figures in them!).

The coach was made from cast Mazac (or Zamac) – an alloy of zinc, aluminium, magnesium, and copper – and the horses were slush cast in lead by Benbros, a small diecasting firm situated a few miles away from Lesney in Gosport Road, Walthamstow, London. Lead was used extensively in toy making, but there was a problem with it. Lead could not be present in the Lesney factory, because if it contaminated their zinc formula, the metal would deteriorate and become unusable. For this reason, any lead components were always sourced elsewhere. With wholesalers Morris and Stone (later Morestone Toys) distributing the coaches in the USA, Benbros making the horses, and Lesney the

The large-scale coronation coach sold 33,000 units in 1953. The miniature version sold over 1 million pieces.

> **The Triumph TT Motorcycle and Sidecar No.4c is rumoured to be Jack Odell's favourite model.**

carriage, it is easy to see how north London diecasting firms collaborated to produce and distribute toys at that time. The large-scale coach was shown at the Harrogate Toy Fair, and no doubt it featured at the Festival of Britain, which marked the beginning of the country's move to pull away from the austerity of post-war Britain and to look to the future. The coach was a huge success, with sales of over one million at £1, 7 shillings and 6 pence each. This took the company turnover to very dizzying heights in those somewhat austere days of 1950s Britain. Lesney soon introduced a scaled-down 1:64 version of the coach, which also sold spectacularly well at 11d each, and this set the company on a path to enormous success.

> **Jack Odell owned a two-tone Vauxhall Cresta which was the inspiration for production of the No.22a model**

No.8a Caterpillar Tractor

The first type in two colourways

No.11a ERF Petrol Tanker

Booty call!

No.11a ERF Petrol Tanker

In three colourways

BEGINNING THE 1-75 RANGE - A NEW ERA

AFTER MUCH SUCCESS with general diecast manufacturing, Lesney wanted to concentrate solely on toy manufacturing, and there are a number of stories about how the first small scale model, the Diesel Road Roller, came about in 1953. An excellent resource for all things Matchbox is Nick Jones's website Vintage British Diecast, where you can find the definitive answer to most questions.

Jack Odell's grandson, James Hanratty, says that Jack's daughter Anne kept bringing home worms and spiders in a disused matchbox from the Norvic Match Company, and Jack posed a question to her: if he were to make a toy to fit in her matchbox, would she stop bringing insects home? She agreed, and Jack made a scaled-down version of the 1947 Road Roller in brass, which was an instant hit with Anne and her school mates.

One of the most fascinating aspects of this stage in the journey of Matchbox toys is the marketing. In the 1950s, smoking was the thing. Grown-ups smoked, cigarette advertising was everywhere, and film stars all seemed to smoke. In London at that time there were over 20 match making businesses, and Bryant & May had been making matches in the capital since the 1840s. Their boxes resemble Lesney's own packaging, but it is said that it was the Czechoslovakian company Norvic from which Lesney took they inspiration for their packaging.

Both firms produced distinctive yellow boxes with black font to hold their products, and these two makers dominated the UK market – so what better vessel to copy to package your product in?

Whilst the packaging was genius, the marketing was exceptional. Initially, before being offered to sweet shops and newsagents, Matchbox toys were only sold in tobacconists, where your smoker (i.e. the majority of the adult population) would pop in for a packet of cigarettes and a box of matches for two shillings. At point of sale, they would be offered a seemingly Norvic Match Company box, but with a beautiful child's toy inside, for just one shilling and six pence. An easy spend to brighten up your child's life!

> Each Matchbox toy cost one shilling and sixpence in the UK and 49 cents in the US

In 1953 came the first of the series in the form of the aforementioned No.1 Road Roller, the No.2 Dumper, and No.3 Cement Mixer. Soon to follow in the year ahead were the No.4 Massey Harris Tractor, No.5 London Bus, No.6 Quarry Truck, and No.7 Horse Drawn Milk Float. Lesney engage Moko to package and market the toys for a percentage of the profit, and eventually the two parties agreed to a 50/50 ownership of the registered mark of Matchbox (more about this later).

Moko at that time was a

Matchbox First Series Box End Types

worldwide distributor of toys, and was able to offer financial services and backing to the relatively newly formed Matchbox toy brand, as they did for many manufacturers of toys.

Following a disagreement with Moko, by 1954 native New Yorker and salesman, Fred Bronner, had become the sole importer for Lesney in the US – a market that was going to prove to be both the champion and the downfall of the brand. They were sold across the entire US at 49 cents apiece, in blister packs to give them maximum visibility. At this time the small factory in Edmonton, London was employing around 70 staff, and it was time for a move to better premises. In 1955, the firm moved to a factory in Shacklewell Lane, Dalston, London, and soon afterwards they acquired a foundry just across the A10 road at Barrett's Grove. Shacklewell became the first toolroom and foundry, and Barrett's Grove was to become the second toolroom, with the addition of a foundry and assembly line. Barrett's Grove was a disused railway sleeper works before Lesney converted it, and coincidentally I used to walk past that very building

> **In 1968 Matchbox Toys won Toy of the Year in the US – stealing a march on the US toy industry**

every month on my way to work meetings without knowing the history of it. Today the development is called Matchbox Yard, and it contains some very swanky apartments (£650,000 for a two-bedroom home). According to Lesley Smith, in his interview with the Hackney Museum, it was the No.5 London Bus which really proved the winner for the company. It was a perfect little model, introduced in 1954, and like many of the early models it was a scaled-down version of a Dinky toy (the 29c Leyland, in this case). Painted in various shades of red, with gold trim to the grille and unpainted diecast wheels, it had the new addition of paper labels to the advertising boards on each side. The labels were yellow with black lettering – "Buy 'Matchbox' Series" – although unlabelled ones were also produced, presumably because they had run out of labels. Around this time the company began to get into their stride with the design, manufacturing, and distribution processes. The construction of Lesney toys has stood the test of time because of the way they were manufactured. They were made from an alloy of 94% zinc, 4% aluminium, and 1% magnesium (each north London diecast toy firm appeared to have a different percentage mix). And even today, over 70 years later, the structure of these models has not deteriorated, which is more than can be said of lot of other similar diecast manufacturers of the day. The axles were made of mild steel, sourced from a local manufacturer initially, and they consisted of a flat head at one end with the other plain end being crimped to hold on the wheels once the assembly was complete. This was the process used for making axles until 1959, when the crimped end was then rounded off using a rivet, presumably for safety reasons. And the company continued with this method until the Superfast era started in 1969.

The dies for each model could be modified very easily to allow for changes to the design. Ejector rings and pips were added to make for easier removal of the toy from the die, and when dies were getting to the end of their working life, replacements were made that were sometimes slightly different to the original die. Weak parts of the toy were strengthened, towing slots were added, and glazing rivets attached, which all makes for an interesting line of models to collect as there are many, many variations to look out for.

The unpainted diecast Mazac wheels were dipped into a formula to turn them grey, and these were used until around 1958 when grey and black plastic wheels were introduced (silver plastic wheels came a little later), and of course there were rubber tracks for some of the commercials. Plastic wheels with a knobbly tread came first, and these were replaced with a finer tread, and by the mid-1960s both the silver and the grey plastic wheels were discontinued. In the 1960s coloured plastic hubs with grey or black plastic wheels were used, along with chromed hubs on some models, and these were all superseded with Superfast wheels at the end of the decade.

As the paint was sourced from a number of outside manufacturers, there was a good deal of colour variation, although most models came in just one colour in the early years. Initially gold trim was applied by hand, and this was later replaced with silver trim until late 1959 when mask spraying was used. This really started to make the manufacturing process more efficient.

The early paper labels were soon replaced with decals which were applied with a solvent, but Jack Odell disliked the mess produced on the factory floor using solvent decals, and these were eventually replaced with a waterslide version.

> **In 1968 100,000 transfers were applied by hand every day**

There are a number of rare variants out there to look out for, where the wrong decals have been applied to a model (mainly buses), although it is definitely a case of 'buyer beware' as these are very easy to fake. With a genuine decal you can feel the raised print on top by running your fingernail over it. Fake decals have the printing underneath the surface, and when you run your fingernail over these, there is no raised printing.

The box making was outsourced in the earlier years, and of course the box design changed slightly, and the box sizes grew eventually as the range evolved – most notably when Lesney parted company with their distribution partner in 1958/9, and the word 'Moko' was dropped.

Lesney supplied toys directly to small stockists in the late 1940s and early 1950s, before they began supplying Woolworth Stores in London for the Christmas season in 1952. Although the company realised there was a high demand for their toys, it was not economically viable for them to employ a sales force to market and sell the product just for a few months at Christmas, so they turned to toy distributors to help them with this.

Moko was a successful and long-standing firm which marketed and distributed toys in the UK and overseas.

They also provided capital for small toy distributors, in return for a percentage of sales. I think it is fair to say Moko took Lesney from a strong and successful local manufacturer of toys to a truly global company. Moko's history is fascinating and worthy of recording here as part of the journey of Matchbox toys.

The firm was founded sometime between 1865 and 1875 (reports vary) in Furth, near Nuremburg, Germany, by Moritz (Moses) Kohnstamm, and the business specialised in packaging, warehousing, distributing, marketing, and financial backing for toy manufacturers. All toys were marketed as Moko toys, regardless of who made them, and it was a hugely successful company established in many major European cities.

In 1880, they co-founded the very influential and successful Manchester Toy Week for wholesalers, and Moritz's son Julius established the company's UK headquarters at 24 Milton Street, London EC2 (which later became Whitbread Brewery's London HQ). Julius ran the London operation until 1953 when he handed the reins to his son Richard. It was Richard who Leslie Smith and Jack Odell dealt with whilst negotiating the distribution deal.

At the outbreak of the First World War, Moko's office in

Milton Street was expropriated by the War Office and used to make munitions parts, before it resumed toy production in 1919. Just before the Second World War, Moritz's son Emil arrived in the UK and established a doll factory in Aylesbury, Buckinghamshire. This was in 1934, and over the next few years the situation in Germany for Jewish families such as the Kohnstamms became very unwelcoming, dangerous, and ultimately murderous.

Using the money generating from the doll factory, Emil bought a number of properties in London and set about a programme to assist Jews fleeing Nazi Germany. Little is known of the numbers saved, but it is yet another stark reminder of how a situation of living harmoniously with others can quickly, in a very short space of time, turn to intolerance and hatred when propaganda and religious and political fervour is involved.

With the Nazi regime in full swing in Germany, all businesses were confiscated from Jewish owners and handed over to the party, and in 1938 Moko's Furth, Nuremburg toy store was seized by the Dresden Bank and sold to Gustav Schickendanz. From 1933 until the end of the war Schickendanz had participated in the 'Aryanisation' of Germany by not only joining the Nazi

Party, but by also purchasing multiple businesses taken from Jewish families. Thankfully, all restitution claims were settled in the period after the war, but the cost in human lives was horrific and well documented.

The sons of Moritz – Willi, Julius, and Emil – left Germany to establish businesses in the UK, and they ultimately survived the persecution of Jews during the Second World War by the Nazis. Sadly, his daughters, Helene and Sophia, were not so fortunate. They both perished in the Ghetto at Lodz in Poland, which must have left a dreadful scar on the emotions of the surviving family.

Moko Toys can be found all over the world in many guises, early toys are very sought after. Moko Lesney toys were distributed worldwide from 1953, and in 1954, when Fred Bronner became the sole importer for the US, this meant that Matchbox toys were available in just about all four corners of the globe. This is still reflected today as there is truly a worldwide network of Matchbox toy collectors from everywhere on earth.

According to Leslie Smith, there had been a disagreement between the two firms of Moko and Lesney regarding the registering of the Matchbox brand as a trademark. Kohnstamm had registered the brand in his name only, without the consent of Leslie and Jack, and of course they were furious when they found out. Following a series of straight-talking meetings and sternly worded letters, Kohnstamm was forced to re-register the brand in the names of all parties.

It was perhaps a very short-sighted act of greed on Kohnstamm's behalf, and one which certainly struck a terminal blow to the business partnership. However, there was also a disagreement regarding the Asian market, as Leslie Smith thought this region – and Japan in particular – could prove very profitable, but Richard Kohnstamm disagreed. Seeing that the business relationship was beginning to fracture, Richard sold his share of the business to Lesney in 1958 for the sum of £80,000. This was an enormous sum – equivalent to £1.3m today – but in buying out Kohnstamm, the company could now forge their own way ahead in the worldwide market for toys.

The first thing the company did was to produce a catalogue of the range of toys available. In his Hackney Museum interview, Leslie Smith gives an interesting insight as to how the 1-75 range came about. As the range grew in size, it became apparent that stockists would not be able to afford the space to stock an infinite number of toys, so it was decided that the range would stop at 75, and new models would replace old models ongoing. At the same time, the business started to look at more overseas markets to sell their toys.

Although Lesney factories had been established in 1956 in Austria and Switzerland, it was the German market that was the first to flourish for them. Jakob Prins was a Dutch toy manufacturer who headed a company called Edor. He bought a former dairy in Rees in North Rhine Westphalia, and acquired the distribution rights for Matchbox in Germany. Shipments of Matchbox toys would come from Hackney, via Rotterdam, and the factory would repackage them and distribute them across Germany. The models were even available in communist East Germany, where such frivolous items would not usually be readily available. The work was mainly carried out by women, as it was in the UK.

By 1959, at home Lesney dominated the landscape in Hackney; there was an enormous factory as well as facilities in other parts of London, along with factories and facilities in 14 other countries across the globe. They were truly at the beginning of something big when construction started in 1962 of their brand new, state-of-the-art, factory complex in Lee Conservancy Road, Hackney, London. The factory took two years to complete, and it added a further 200,000 square feet to the already enormous factory space across the borough. Most of the new machinery needed to produce the toys was designed by Jack Odell himself, and each machine was built and installed by Lesney's own engineers. Having designed, made, and installed the machinery themselves, the production of their toys would be cheaper and more efficient than their rivals.

Not only was Jack a great engineer, but he was also creative and technically minded. He was truly a genuine manufacturer to the core. For example, he designed a machine for automatically fitting tyres to wheels: two containers, one held tyres, the other held wheels, and the mechanics of the machinery fitted tyres to wheels at a rate of 7,000 per minute. Jack also made a machine for pressure spraying tiny headlamps to cars, and to make one-piece moulds for interiors, as well as a myriad other inventions. He was a true engineering genius.

Leslie's role was to grow and steer the company. He organised the plants needed to make the toys and recruited the staff needed to do the job. He was the numbers man, skilled at maximising profit for the company. But he was also principled, as both he and Jack refused to move production to the much cheaper Far

East because they believed in keeping British jobs. Even after he left Lesney, he was still making a financial difference when he acted as a governor of St Paul's School in Winchmore Hill, London, and took it out of deep debt to a £500,000 bank balance within a small number of years. Together Jack and Leslie were the perfect partnership for the business, complimenting each other brilliantly.

As well as soaring sales at home and in Europe, Matchbox in the US also sold phenomenally well; a great price point at 49c each, the toys were very affordable, and played with and loved by the children of one of the biggest nations in the world. In 1964, Lesney Products (US) was formed, with Fred Bronner as president, and in 1969 the company became Lesney Products Corporation. In 2010, I was fortunate enough to visit the HQ in NYC at 120, East 23rd Street, and although the company and all trace of it is long gone, above street level you can see how wonderful and imposing the 1930s building is totally fitting as the US HQ for a global company. In the following years, further factories were acquired in London and Essex, and a Spray Shop was added to

By 1966 Lesney had sold 500m Matchbox toys worldwide

the newly built Lee Conservancy Road site, enabling the weekly production run to exceed 5 million toys, and the workforce topping 7,000 people by the end of 1969.

No.12a Land Rover

Featured a more detailed grille

No.13a Bedford Wreck Truck

No.13b has a longer flat top edge

No.14a Daimler Ambulance

No.17a Removals Vans

3 of 4 colourways

No.17a Removals Vans

3 of 4 colourways, three is the magic number

GLOBAL EXPANSION

AS THE FIRM GREW and production increased, the business was soon arranged over various departments. The seeds of a new model were planted in the Research & Development department, where a small team would work on the viability of the model. Meetings with senior management and sales personnel were then held on a Tuesday to agree on which design to choose for the next model. Only the best were approved for production, and there must have been a certain amount of disappointment amongst the team if their preferred model wasn't accepted. Once agreed, the department would approach the manufacturer of the real, full sized vehicles for photographs, dimensions, etc. Sometimes new toy cars were on the Lesney drawing board before the real car was even launched.

Once the new model was accepted, it went over to the

> **In 1966 most Matchbox Toys produced were sold abroad: 9% in London, 11% to the rest of the UK and 80% to the rest of the world.**

Drawing Office, where a team of designers and draughtsmen were tasked with producing the design of all new models which had been approved at the R&D meetings. This task often took many hours to complete. Once the design was approved, it would be sent over to the Pattern Shop, where a team of highly skilled and specialised Pattern Makers and Model Makers, along with Project Engineers, would carve a large wooden scale model from which the casts would eventually be made. The finished wooden models were then taken to the Tool Shop, where a team of over 100 toolmakers produced the casts to make the toys, using top grade chrome-vanadium steel.

Jack Odell was notoriously hands on, and he insisted on perfection. He would often take over from a toolmaker if he felt things weren't quite right, and he was, by all accounts, constantly on the shop floor checking for quality.

Lesney employed not only thousands of production line operatives, but also hundreds of very skilled engineers. In total there were over 150 specialist diecasting machines, which had all been designed, made, and installed in-house. It is said that when the first automatic diecast machine was turned on by Jack, the rest of the workforce had fled, fearing the machine would burst, spewing molten metal everywhere. It didn't, obviously!

After the cast had been perfected, the diecasting machines produced the many thousands of models which were then fettled to remove any snagged bits of metal. Then it was off to the Paint Shop, where machines were designed to spray models quickly. A series of rotating posts were designed for an individual model to be placed on top, and as the model passed through the paint booth on a conveyor, it would be automatically sprayed in the chosen colour.

Lesney had managed to source a unique lead-free paint from Australia which would be used to spray hundreds of thousands of models a day. The final part of the process, known as stove enamelling, involved baking the paint on at very high temperatures.

> **In the 1960s Matchbox used 2,000 gallons of lead-free paint per week.**

It is worth labouring the point that Jack was of course an engineering genius, inventing just about everything needed in the process of toy manufacture. The previously mentioned tyre machine would feed one of each of the components to a section which forced the tyre onto the hub, in readiness for the entire wheel to be fitted to the axle by hand. Because the machine could do this at a rate of so many thousands an hour, it saved an awful lot of human resource and time, and it must have saved the company a lot in terms of production costs.

It wasn't long before Lesney established their own plastics department, which produced more and more components for the models (from the beginning of the 1960s onwards), and there were eventually as many plastic components to produce as there were diecast ones.

Lesney used tin biscuit boxes from Huntley & Palmers to transport component parts around the factory, which was both inexpensive and efficient. There were hundreds of conveyors moving these 15-inch square tins on overhead and ground floor belts, and in excess of 20 production lines in action at the Hackney factory. Every department used these tins, from diecasting through to the production line, and if you ever see one come up for sale, you should buy it because they are very valuable items indeed.

Each line was staffed by hundreds of local women, the Lesney Ladies, who would be tasked with fitting components to models as they came down the line. It might not always have been the same model that needed components added; often several models would be on the production line at any one time, each requiring their specific components.

There is anecdotal evidence that on Fridays, when the various teams had come back to the line from the traditional drink at the local pub, mistakes were made. Some models received the wrong components, wrong decals were applied, or correct ones were applied in the wrong position, and sometimes the wrong wheels were applied. Occasionally, these models would be missed during quality checking, or they would otherwise be rejected into the bin, but some managed to get out of the factory. And it is these models which are highly prized today; any one of them would be a truly valued addition to any collection.

As you can imagine, accuracy and speed was necessary on the production line, and the company paid generous bonuses for the workers producing the best quality models whilst still hitting their production target. Lesney were, by all accounts, quite hard taskmasters, and the Lesney Ladies caught the brunt of it. For example, they were only allowed a one-minute break to use the lavatory, and some would use this time ingeniously, by making every second count.

Nick Jones (British Vintage Diecast) interviewed one such worker, who told him how she turned her loo break into a cigarette break too; she would light up a cigarette, run up the stairs to the loo, and smoke as much of what she could of her cigarette in that time. On entering the loos, she handed the rest of it over to a colleague to finish in their loo break. It wasn't just Jack who was inventive and efficient, it seems!

Despite having strict quality controls, towards the end of a production run things could become a bit fraught. For example, if the correct paint for a model ran out, they would use an alternative shade in order to finish the run. Or if the red painted hooks for the No.13 Wreck Truck were not finished, they would use unpainted ones, etc. This would result in some slightly varied models, and it is all these anomalies which make Matchbox toy collecting so fascinating, with endless variants of the same model.

Once the model was completed and off the production line, it needed to be packed into the iconic match boxes. But Lesney didn't produce their own boxes for Matchbox toys; this was contracted out to another iconic business nearby.

William Bowater established himself as a newsprint agent in London in 1881, before establishing a very successful paper manufacturing business, which for a period of time was the sole, worldwide provider of newsprint. In 1924, Bowater built a large mill on the river Thames dockside at Northfleet, Kent, which produced newsprint and paper products for companies across the globe. In 1956, Bowater-Scott was formed, and for a period of time this company made the Matchbox toy boxes.

Lesney did, of course, design their own boxes, and once the boxes came back from the printers, they were almost ready to have the models inserted into them.

Jack designed an ingenious machine which handled the flat packed boxes, picked them up, shaped them, and closed the flaps at one end ready for the laborious task of placing a toy inside (which was of course performed by the Lesney Ladies at a rate of 120 per minute, per person). Once finished, the products were finally packed into boxes of 72, ready to leave the factory, destined for toy shops around the globe.

Just like the Bowater boxes, most raw materials came in from nearby factories in London. Zinc came by canal and arrived at the Eastway Zinc Alloy Company, which adjoined the Lesney canalside factory (98% of Eastway's production went to Lesney). Before Matchbox made their own plastics, these too came from a number of local London factories. It was the unique lead-free paint which travelled the most distance, having been sourced initially from Australia.

> **When Lesney took over distribution from Moko they were able to reduce the price per toy in Germany from 1.75DM to 1DM; thus making Germany the biggest European market for their toys.**
> **And today Germany is still the biggest European market for Matchbox Toy collectors.**

The company began to grow and exceed all expectations, and by 1966 Lesney had become very successful at exporting their products. By then, only 9% of toys were sold to London shops, with 11% going to the rest of the UK stockists, and a massive 80% going to the nearby docks for export all around the world. Whilst this is a great mix of business to have when the UK pound is weaker, any strengthening of the UK pound will see a sharp drop in profits, making it a bit of a gamble.

However, Lesney continued to produce a vast quantity of toys – up to 5.5m per week at their peak in the late 1960s – and throughout the entire decade they succeeded in innovating and producing toys on a vast scale. As the largest employer in the Borough of Hackney, they

Staff Bus

had various issues regarding parking; their own car park became full to capacity, and with various shifts to cover and not wanting staff to rely on local buses, they had to think of a solution. As well as the need to resolve

The employee bus service used between 20 and 30 of mainly RT and RHL buses. Initially painted blue with the yellow Matchbox logo to the advertising boards, they were later resprayed in Superfast colours of orange, yellow and white.

Staff Bus

Staff Bus

the parking problem, the company also needed to recruit a constant supply of personnel for the production line as the business grew bigger each month. The solution came in the form of company buses.

Lesney bought an entire fleet of used AEC London buses, repainted them in the blue and yellow colours of their boxes, and offered a service which picked up their workforce and returned them at the end of their shift. Most of the production line workforce used the free bus service, which was timetabled around the various shifts being operated, and it became a much-loved service by those who used it.

It was a real winner for the company, too, because it made for a more reliable workforce and added to the desire to control the production process from beginning to end, which makes economic sense. A number of ex-employees, who were interviewed for the Hackney Museum's exhibition some years ago, said there was often a mad scramble at the end of the shift to get packed up and on the bus before it left, and that often non- Lesney staff would hitch a ride on the buses as a free trip to their place of work! Some drivers would also be willing to drop employees off at their home if they could, and to show their gratitude the Ladies would arrange a whip round on payday for each driver.

Such was the success of Lesney's exports, they won several industry awards, the most prestigious being the Queen's Award for Inustry, which they first applied for and won in 1966.

> **The company was awarded the Queen's Award for Export in 1966, 1968 and 1969; every employee got a bonus to celebrate, and Leslie Smith, by then a millionaire, was appointed OBE in 1968.**

In 1968, there was a huge award ceremony when the Queen's Lieutenant Sir Gerald Templer presented the award to the company, and each member of staff was given a piece of Lesney Giftware to mark the occasion.

The following year, and with the Royal Standard flying high over the factory, on 12th November, 1969, Queen Elizabeth II arrived by helicopter to inspect the factory, escorted on the tour by Jack and Leslie. This must have been a very special moment for both men, having fought for King and country decades earlier then gone on to establish a world leader in diecast toy manufacturing. They must have felt very proud.

The Queen was given a gift of a Superfast track and models for the then nine-year-old Prince Andrew (I wonder if he still has them, or if he has sold them on eBay?!). The company also featured in the Guinness Book of Records in 1967 for producing 100 million models annually. A little later, they were employing over 6,000 local people in full and part-time work. These are big numbers and great achievements from a company that started off in the basement of a bombed-out pub.

Lesney outshone their competitors, including the likes of Mattoy (Corgi) and Scalextric in the UK, and they were voted the best toy manufacturer in the US (which was their main export source, followed by Germany and Japan).

Leslie and Jack were also awarded the OBE in 1968. For them, it was the pinnacle of their careers, as they rode high on their fame and fortune. Jack always said he wanted to be a millionaire by the time he was 40, which he says he achieved with just days to spare. And indeed, he bought a £200,000 house in north London in 1974 (equivalent to £2.1m today) which had room on the driveway for his beloved Aston Martin.

> **Number of countries exported to = 130**

No.17c Austin Taxi

A handsome model

No.19a MG Midget

In cream, missing the tan driver

No.20a ERF Stake Truck

No.21a Bedford Coach

No.22a 1956 Vauxhall Cresta

Also available in lighter red

No.23a Berkeley Cavalier Caravan

This model had no number to the base

No.25a Bedfordd Dunlop Van

No.26a ERF Cement Mixer

One of many early ERF models

No.26a ERF Cement Mixer

No.27a Bedford Low Loader

Look out for the blue variant

THE WORKFORCE

IT IS OFTEN SAID it was a loyal and happy workforce that worked for Lesney, and certainly they had many employees who worked for the company for decades. But this was a time when conditions for workers were largely unregulated and often poor in comparison to what we enjoy today. Women were paid much less than men for doing the same work, and no women held any senior or skilled roles at Lesney in the 1960s.

> **On the production line Lesney Ladies were tasked to pack 120 toys per minute**

Former staff often say it was friendly and like one big happy family, with good pay and a non-contributory pension, and that it was the sort of place where you made friends for life. It was fiercely non-unionised, as the CEOs and the Executives were very anti-union – if you did something wrong you were sacked, according to one ex-employee. But like all large employers of its time, it wasn't the case that everybody was happy.

It has been said by an ex-production line worker, in an

interview for the Hackney Museum project, that before the Race Relations Act, Jack Odell would not allow non-white employees at the plant. Whilst this is anecdotal evidence, the employee did note that although the community in Hackney in the 1960s was diverse, with people whose heritage was from all around the world, the Lesney workforce did not reflect the community at large, which is sadly indicative of the attitude of that era.

When the Race Relations Act was introduced in 1965, no employer in the UK could discriminate against people on grounds of colour, race, ethnicity, or national origin, which meant everybody had to be treated equally from the interview process through to retirement. This certainly meant that Lesney began to employ people from all backgrounds, and the workforce then began to representing the community better. With this in mind, the previously mentioned production line employee stated that everybody seemed to work well together.

In my research for this book, I found some information about a very interesting woman employed by Lesney, who I had learned about years ago during my study of political history. Astrid Proll had joined the Red Army Faction in Germany, which was a group opposed to imperialism and opposed to Nazis in West Germany.

Two of its members, Andreas Baader and Ulrike Meinhof, had been arrested for their involvement in an arson attack at a Frankfurt department store. But whilst being held, awaiting trial, they escaped from jail with help from members of the group. Astrid was the driver for the getaway, and she also became the driver in a series of bank robberies that were to follow.

Now a wanted woman, the search for Astrid began, and she was eventually captured. Whilst awaiting trial, she was held in solitary confinement in a special cell which was painted entirely in brilliant white, with a bare neon strip light on 24/7. There was no discernible natural light and the cell was impenetrable to noise. This amounted to tortuous life, which she endured for two years, and which directly resulted in the deterioration of her mental and physical health at the young age of 24.

In 1974 her trial was adjourned because of her ill health, and she was granted bail. Whilst on bail, she fled West Germany and arrived in London in August 1974. Astrid was looked after by people sympathetic to her political activism, and she worked several jobs whilst living near the Lesney factory in Hackney. She enrolled in a Borough-funded training course held at the Poplar Skill

Centre, where she trained as a car mechanic and obtained a City and Guilds certificate in mechanics and welding. Whilst in London, she also passed her driving test, got a national insurance card, and became a member of a trade union.

Later in 1974, Astrid started work as a Fitter's Mate at the Lesney factory. However, she was ostracised by fellow employees for a number of reasons, it appears. There was much anger towards her because she was a woman doing a man's job. Some men refused to work with her, she was treated with suspicion, and she was given hateful nicknames. In particular, one supervisor really made things bad for her by attempting to make life so difficult that she would leave. But it evidently didn't work, as Astrid joined the Amalgamated Electrical Union, continued to work hard, and eventually gained a supervisor role.

Astrid was eventually arrested and deported to Germany, where she remained in jail despite many local and national campaigns to raise money for her and to free her. She was sentenced to 5 years imprisonment for her role as getaway driver, but because she had spent three of those years awaiting trial, she was released immediately.

She now works as a lecturer based in Germany, and is far removed from her brief spell at Lesney and Baader Meinhof all those years ago.

No.28a Bedford Compressor Truck

Showing excellence in detailed diecasting

No.30a Ford Prefect

Also in rare sky blue

No.31a American Ford Station Wagon

No.32a Jaguar XK140

Two beauties, one orange-red, one white

No.33a Ford Zodiac

Available in many other colours

No.34a Volkswagon Van

WORKFORCE RELATIONS AND CONDITIONS

IT IS FAIR TO SAY that if you worked for Lesney, you had landed a very good job. It was the biggest employer in the Borough of Hackney, providing vital income to many working-class women who accounted for two-thirds of the workforce.

Number of Staff in the mid-1960s = 6,000

Whether you were a 16-year-old working a holiday job, or a senior toolmaker, or designer, the pay and benefits were above average, but there were a few inequities which were fairly standard for the era, and Lesney had their own way of doing things which sometimes seemed unfair. Jack Odell was very 'hands on', and he would constantly check the work being carried out by his staff. He would even take over a job if he thought it wasn't being carried out correctly, which might seem like micro-management today. However, on occasions, quality gave way to quantity as production targets needed to be met. As previously mentioned, different shades of colour were substituted if the original was out of stock, or if the right component was unavailable it would be substituted for something else – something that Jack probably would not have approved of.

This was an era when pay and conditions were better for men than for women (and remember, women made up the vast majority of the workforce), but Lesney was one of few local employers who offered a large range of employee benefits. There was a non-contributory pension, shift work which paid better wages than standard hours, bonuses if production and other targets were achieved, a staff canteen (which Jack used to eat in, rather than use the executive facilities), free transport to and from work, gifts when the company did well and won awards, a social club, a fooball team, and a 30-minute lunch break.

I have the employment file for one member of staff who worked in the Export Sales Team in 1967, when the average office/sales wage was £884 (equivalent to £19,000 today). His basic salary was £1100 (£24,000 today) and he had a Ford Cortina 1600L as a company car, which was a very smart thing indeed. He even wrote to the directors of the company to ask for a promotion when the Export Sales Manager left, which gives us some idea as to how accessible the board of directors were (he got a reply back and was awarded the promotion!).

In the 1960s, pay and conditions were different for men and women, where men's benefits exceeded those of women. As completion of the new Lee Conservatory Road factory drew nearer, Lesney started to see women leaving. It seemed that they were not keen on the idea of working en masse in large industrial factory facilities, preferring the existing arrangement of working in small groups. The company needed to do something to retain staff.

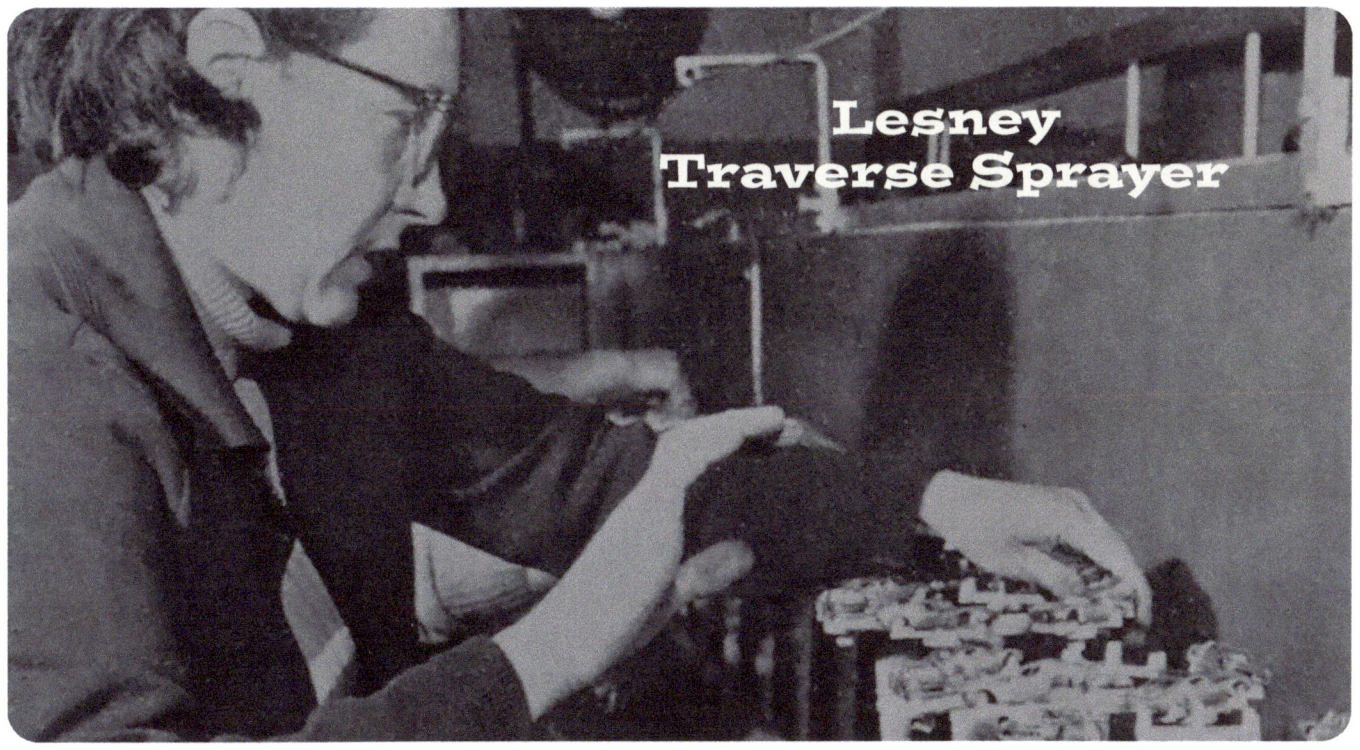

One of the ways Lesney managed to entice workers back and retain employees was to offer shift work of 10am to 3pm to fit around parenting, and to introduce the free bus service. The bus service, as outlined in the company handbooks, was 'strictly for women only', although now and again, men did get onboard if they knew the driver. However, the company non-contributory pension, which was unusual for the time and would have been a very valuable benefit, was only available to men – that was the norm at the time.

Lesney was also a non-unionised business, which some may argue was detrimental to the workforce. Each section had a Staff Representative who employees could go to with any issues. However, if you stepped out of line or your work wasn't up to scratch, you could quite easily and very swiftly be dismissed.

> **In 1967 Lesney, with the help of its largely female workforce, was awarded its place in The Guinness Book of Records when its annual output reached 100 million models and by 1969 output had soared to a million units a day.**

When unions were allowed at the firm in the 1970s, the union which represented them was the Amalgamated Union of Engineering Workers. However, it was run by men and had a membership consisting almost entirely of men, with women not supported nor represented. In any case, Lesney chose not to deal with unions and continued to negotiate via the Staff Representatives. It was to be a few years before equal pay for both sexes was mandatory, and even then, to get around the legislation where men and women doing the same job must be on the same pay, Lesney separated the men and women out and maintained women only and men only roles and pay scales. This was undoubtedly common practice in industry at the time, although it is of course totally discriminatory.

There were very few incidents of industrial action at Lesney, which may be an indicator that employer/employee relations were nearly always harmonious. However, there was one prominent incident when, in April 1975, an unfair dismissal case was heard at an industrial tribunal which made it into UK case law. Lesney employed Machine Setters who set the machines, maintained them, and ensured they were all working correctly. They were employed over both day and night shifts, and the role was heavily dependent on overtime – all very costly for the employer at a time when toy sales were diminishing. Lesney restructured the work into two separate day shifts, hence cutting out the expensive night shift and overtime pay, but retained all 36 men. However, their pay had effectively been reduced from

£70 per week to £54 per week, which is equivalent today of reducing a salary from £29,000 to £22,000.

Some men refused to accept the terms and pay, and they were dismissed. Following dismissal, they argued that redundancy awards were payable under the circumstances. However, it was adjudged by Lord Denning that they had not been made redundant, as the company had still offered them employment following the restructure and pay reduction, but they had voluntarily left their roles. So their redundancy claims were dismissed.

There is one other incident of poor employee relations which is notable in Lesney's history, and which also occurred in the 1970s. In 1965, the Race Relations Act was the first piece of legislation to address discrimination on the grounds of colour, race, or ethnic or national origins, and in the workplace this meant that businesses could not refuse to employ anyone because of their ethnicity.

In 1975, an ex-employee of Ugandan heritage returned to the Lesney offices in pursuit of work, but she was told there were no jobs available. Upon leaving the offices, she saw a notice advertising the job she had enquired about. Feeling excluded and upset by this, she approached the

Race Relations Board for advice.

A case worker at the Race Relations Board, who had a 'BBC British' accent, telephoned the same office at Lesney to enquire about the job role the ex-employee had asked about, and was told there was indeed work available for her.

When Lesney were approached by the Board about this, they advised that the woman had left her job of her own free will in the first instance, and they appeared to be irked enough that she now wanted to come back not to re-employ her. They also pointed out that they employed many people from ethnic backgrounds, although it was evident they did not want this particular employee back, without giving any explanation as to their reasons.

The case was tested in a court of law and, whilst the outcome has not been recorded, unless Lesney did give a reasonable explanation for not wishing to have the employee back, which was not based upon her colour, race, or ethnic origin, I cannot see how the company could have won the case.

It has to be said that, aside from nationwide industrial action and a small skirmish involving the Fettling team, the above examples are the only two documented examples of unrest at Lesney's in their entire history, which is remarkable. Unfortunately, though, all these difficult circumstances seem to have come at the same time for the company.

The early to mid-1970s had been a tough few years for Lesney, as there had been a series of setbacks other than the court cases already mentioned. In 1973, there was an eight-week general strike, and following this the workers in the Fettling department went on strike. Then the Rochford factory, which made Models of Yesteryear, caught fire, and a short time afterwards it then flooded, which halted production of the models for almost two years.

Having suffered so many setbacks, this was undoubtedly a tough spell for the company, but to conclude, these were the only production difficulties documented. Lesney had relatively few employee relations issues, and where there are records and interviews of ex-employees for various projects, they indicate that the vast majority of the staff enjoyed working for the company.

No.35a ERF Marshall Horsebox

No.37a Karrier Bantum Coca-Cola Truck

No.38a Karriaer Bantam Refuse Trucks

Grey and silver (also available in brown)

No.39a Ford Zodiac Convertable

No.42a Bedford Evening News Van

Beautiful from evevry angle

No.42a Bedford Evening News Van

The master of detailed decals

No.42a Bedford Evening News Van

No.43a Hillman Minx

Thw all-green variant iis rare

A CHALLENGER THE PERFECT STORM

LESNEY'S MASSIVE EXPANSION was due mainly to their global reach. The business realised early on that there was an enormous market for their brand across the world, which they quickly exploited, setting up factories and distribution centres in many countries. For most of the time in the early years, the toys were manufactured in Hackney, London, and sent to authorised distributors where the models would be packed in traditional Matchbox boxes by local workers.

> **At peak production Lesney made 5.5m toys a week**

One such facility was in Rees in Northrhine-Westfalia, Germany. As touched on earlier Jakob Prins, the founder of Dutch toy company Edor, in 1959 set up a distribution centre on a disused farm and went on to buy the rights to distribute Matchbox toys in Germany. The company received huge containers of toys from London, via Rotterdam, which were then re-packaged by a team of 70 women and distributed across West Germany. There were also special German models in the Superfast range, where several models were re-branded with German company logos (adding yet more variants for today's avid collector).

Lesney also had early distribution partners in other countries. In 1956, Waldmeier AG held the rights for Switzerland and Austria, and there were distribution facilities in Japan, South America, the Commonwealth countries, and even in some Communist countries. However, the main overseas market was with the mighty Lesney Products Corporation headed by Fred Bronner in the US.

By the end of 1969, Lesney were employing over 6,000 people in London, and they were producing 5,500,000 models per week within the various factory complexes. These models were being distributed to 130 countries worldwide, with the US taking a massive 40% of the production.

But during 1966/7, another toy company in the US was developing a new and exciting diecast vehicle range that was to play a major part in the downfall of the Matchbox brand.

Elliot Handler was born in the US in 1916, and in 1945 he and his business partner Harold Matson set up the toy manufacturer Mattel (the brand name was formed from their own names Harold Matson and Elliot Handler). They started by making picture frames in Elliot's garage, then dolls house furniture from the offcuts of wood, and soon became a hugely successful toy manufacturer producing what today are seen as iconic toys.

Mattel was already a giant in the toy industry by the 1960s, and probably Elliot Handler's most famous invention during that time were the Ken & Barbie dolls, which were named after his son Kenneth and his daughter Barbara.

In 1966, Elliot noticed his grandchildren playing with Matchbox cars, but he soon realised they didn't go as fast as his grandchildren wanted them to go when they raced them around the house. This got him thinking about how he could improve upon what was already the top-selling diecast toy brand in the US. Being an inventor, he started to design a new style of diecast toy, and soon the Mattel Research and Development team were put into full action. Elliot saw that kids wanted to play with the toy version of up-to-the-minute, real life cars they would see cruising the streets of California. At that time California was the home of the custom car, and it was these vehicles that Elliot realised drew the attention of children, with their beefed-up engines, jacked suspension, and bright paintwork.

Key to the speed of these new pumped-up Californian cars were the friction-less wheels, where a system was developed using piano gauge wire for axles which allowed for better suspension, and this was lubricated and coupled with a plastic bearing. To assist the speed across the kitchen floor, wide plastic wheels were developed that gave better surface contact, and initially a low friction plastic was used for the bushing between the wheel and the axle. This resulted in the car flying along the prototype plastic tracks Mattel were using to develop the models. These race tracks were also key to the success of the toys, as it was envisaged these could be sold separately as part of a complex, snap-together system of tracks, jumps, and curves that kids could race their cars along.

The diecast bodies were highly polished to an almost mirror shine before a translucent coloured paint was spray applied. This process, known as Spectraflame, gave a candy-coloured metallic finish which had never been achieved before in toy cars, and it made the models extremely eye-catching to the eagle-eyed kids with money to spend.

So now the designers had produced a toy which had a specially developed, super-fast wheel and axle system, a newly invented metallic mirror finish, and each model was designed as a custom hot rod that kids would see in the streets of California: up-to-the-minute models to be released as soon as the real thing was (the Custom Corvette was allegedly released before General Motors launched the real thing at the 1968 Motor Show).

It is the subject of legend that Elliot Handler met with Harry Bentley Bradley to talk business before he joined Mattel. Harry worked for General Motors as a car designer, and Elliot wanted him on board to design for Mattel. After their meeting, and as they were leaving, Elliot spotted Harry's classic El Camino hot rod parked outside and is quoted as commenting, "Man, those are some hot wheels." The rest, as they say, is history.

After much development, Mattel's Hot Wheels were introduced on 18th May, 1968, to the New York Toy Fair – a global event where the latest toy inventions were presented to worldwide toy distributors and where Matchbox toys would be prominently featured. At the same time, Mattel embarked upon an enormous $10,000,000 advertising campaign featuring the new line-up of 16 Californian custom cars (now known as the

Sweet Sixteen) being raced along various trick, jump, and race sets by excited young children. Also featured in these ads were the collectors' metal pin badges, featuring each model, and which could be worn to further advertise Mattel's cars.

In the first 1968 ad, there is also a carry case for the cars which could be bought separately; this added extra play value and extra revenue streams for Mattel. Because of their extremely high play use, a high proportion of Hot Wheels that have survived from that era are extremely playworn today. They truly were 'the fastest miniature metals cars you've seen'.

I could not find any Matchbox US TV ads for 1968 during my research for this book. So, it could be that Lesney didn't see the value of TV ads at a time when they had nothing to rival Mattel's new offering.

In any case, this left Mattel open to flood the airwaves unchallenged with ads for Hot Wheels, and these ads reached the homes of almost every child in the US. In 1968, there were around 200,000,000 people living in the US, and 95% of households had a TV. In that year, US broadcasters had switched to entirely colour programming, therefore approximately 190,000,000 people would see these ads in glorious colour. Contrast this to the UK at the time: ITV was the only channel offering ads, and these were still in black and white, while only about 75% of the population had access to a TV (41,000,000 people). In 1968, the BBC was still king, and its programming was watched almost exclusively by the majority of the UK population. Many households were still very sniffy about watching commercial TV. I had several friends at the time who were not allowed to watch any ITV programmes or adverts, as these households only watched BBC1 or BBC2. The first models were made in the US, but Mattel quickly realised the benefits of manufacturing in the Far East, and in 1969 manufacturing was beginning to switch to Hong Kong. The stage was now set for a showdown in toy sales: newly designed hot rod cars, special super-fast wheels, vibrant colours, racetracks and added accessories, pin/button badges, and a nationwide advertising campaign reaching millions of kids. The perfect storm was brewing.

> **Dunlop was the first company to pay for advertising on a Lesney vehicle (the No.25a Bedford Van)**

No.46a Morris Minor 1000

No.47a Trojan Brooke Bond Tea Van

No.50a Commer MK VIII Pickup

No.51a Albion Chieftain Portland Cement Truck

No.56a London Trolley Bus

No.56a London Trolley Bus

56a London Trolley Bus

No.57a Wolseley 1500

No.59a Ford Thames Singer Van

No.60a Morris J2 Pickup Builder's Van

HOT WHEELS IMPACT

IN MAY 1968, WHEN HOT WHEELS were launched upon the US nation, Lesney's toy sales dropped from $28m to $6m almost overnight. This would have represented almost a 40% drop in the company's overall sales, and I cannot imagine the atmosphere in Fred Bronner's offices in New York City and at home in Hackney, London.

Back in the UK at that time, both Leslie Smith and Jack Odell were awarded the OBE and were the recipients of the first of a number of Queen's Awards for Industry (with a massive 79% of sales being exported when the average was around 24% at the time).

In the moment when the company was riding high, there was increased competition at home as well as abroad when Mettoy introduced their Husky range as direct competition to Matchbox, and the new Budgie toys were introduced in the same scale. Whilst the introduction of UK competitors didn't have much of a detrimental effect on sales, they came at a time of crisis for Lesney, when other factors were also at play. As previously mentioned, the workplace was also changing with legislation being introduced around working practices and race relations, and as working practices changed, jobs were lost.

Around the same time that Hot Wheels were introduced in the US, another competitor entered the market to add yet more pressure on Matchbox sales. The Johnny Lightning range was introduced by Topper Toys of Elizabeth, New Jersey, USA in 1969, almost immediately after Hot Wheels came to market. The company was already a powerhouse in toy manufacturing in the US, producing Suzy and Dawn dolls, and the company already had the resources in place to develop a diecast car range.

The range consisted of 15 models – 14 were models of real cars of the era, and they produced one concept car. Just like Mattel, they designed their range with bright metallic paints with red line type wheels, and children could invest in all sorts of accessories like speed tracks, helmets, and carry cases. As speed was the most important factor in order to compete with Hot Wheels, the designers incorporated a loop under the front axle so that the toy could be propelled by a lever-driven catapult. This made them as quick as lightning, especially as the loop was also designed to engage with a hook on the Johnny Lightning 500 Track Set which propelled the toys around the track like rockets.

Topper Toys marketed these toys as 'The Challenger' and used phrases likes 'Beats Them All' in their campaign to grab a slice of the pie. They were displayed at retailers in blister packs, right alongside Hot Wheels cars. They were designed truly as a direct competitor to Hot Wheels, and it took a little less than 12 months from concept to launch, which was exceedingly quick. This meant that they hit the market several months before Lesney's new offering was available – a valuable head start in the very competitive toy industry.

Whilst Topper Toys went into receivership two years later, in 1971, they managed in a very short space of time to put a serious dent into Mattel's sales of Hot Wheels. But more worryingly for Lesney, it was further and quite devasting competition f Matchbox toys, as the bottom fell out of their market in the US almost overnight.

It was clear that Lesney must act fast to head off Mattel, or suffer the consequences. Money had to found quickly to develop a new range to rival these new thin axled beauties that Mattel, Topper, and other manufacturers in the US were using, and new smooth-running wheels needed to be designed. So Lesney borrowed the enormous sum at the time of £1.5m and the design team was quickly put into action, working long hours and weekends developing the wheels and axles. The transition of almost the entire range from regular wheels and axles to the new type of wheel cost millions of pounds to develop, and millions of pounds were lost in sales revenue whilst Mattel stole the market. These were very tough times.

The new Superfast design that Lesney came up with used 0.6mm steel wire for axles, which were less than half the diameter of the previous regular wheel axles. Thinner wheels were developed using a new grade of plastic, which were then fitted to the thin axles to form a pairing, and this was then clipped into a plastic suspension strip. The suspension strip was then riveted to the base of the model. Because each suspension strip was unique to the length and width of each toy, this took an enormous amount of resources to develop fully, in terms of cash and working hours.

New tooling and machinery were designed and installed, and gradually most of the range of 1-75 were converted to the new Superfast wheels and axles, and the new style boxes were designed and printed to accommodate them. A small part of the range was not converted to Superfast: the Ford and Case tractors, Claas Combine

Harvester, Hay Trailer, and Alvis Stalwart. A further ten models were deemed unsuitable for conversion to Superfast and were deleted from the Matchbox catalogue altogether in 1969.

It was decided that the biggest selling toys in terms of sales volume would be the ones to convert to the new wheels, and these were the 11D Scaffold Truck, 14D Iso Grifo, 15D Volkswagen 1500, 33C Lamborghini Miura, and 41C Ford GT. Personally, at that stage in my life, I was still collecting obsolete Matchbox toys from the 1950s, which was to remain the case until about 1973/4 when I bought my first Superfast (the No.6 Mercedes 350sl). I didn't have much interest in the new toys, and I wonder how many other children of my era didn't take to the new Superfasts either. My view is that it could well have been the next generation who were enthralled by the new fast and furious diecasts.

The transition to Superfast in late 1969 and 1970 was an interesting period, and it produced a few much sought-after models. Some models transitioned to Superfast wheels but kept their original colour schemes for short periods of time before new brighter or metallic paintwork was applied. Models such as the 12C Land Rover Safari in blue and 22C Pontiac GP Coupe in red are certainly ones to look out for (but beware of fakes!). As ever, very valuable models include the pre-production models with silver hubbed wheels made in solid plastic, as the Superfast wheels that were to be put into full production were hollowed out.

Just in time for Christmas 1969, a number of new Superfast models became available in the shops. These were the 5E Lotus Europa, 20D Lamborghini Marzal, 35C Merryweather Fire Engine, 56C BMC 1800 Pininfarina, and the 69C Rolls Royce Silver Shadow Coupe. These were shipped in their millions to the US to compete with Hot Wheels, but as this was over 18 months since Hot Wheels had decimated the US market for Matchbox, was it too little too late?

From 1970 onwards, Lesney went full steam ahead in the production of Superfasts. Cars, vans, and trucks were replaced with fantasy hot rods and dragsters which rolled off the production lines in their multi-millions. In 1971, the Lesney Corporation in the US ran an advertising campaign for kids to swap their old wheels for the new Superfast range. You could take your old, broken Matchbox Regular Wheels model to the toy shop and swap it for a brand new, blister packed Superfast model for the reduced price of 59c.

I shall not go into any further detail regarding Superfasts as this is a whole book in itself (to be covered later), but suffice to say that the switch had been made from the regular wheels to Superfast wheels and a new era had begun for Lesney. And for a while sales soared and the company was back in the game again overseas.

No.64a Scammell Breakdown Truck

No.66a Citroen DS19

No.69a Commer Nestle Van

No.69a Commer Nestle Van

No.70a Ford Thames Estate Car

No.72 Fordson Major Tractor

THE DREADED 1970's AND 1980's

GRADUALLY MATCHBOX TOYS regained some market share with the introduction of new lines, including Rola-Matics (with moving parts) and the brightly tampo'd Streakers in the 1-75 range, and also new larger scale models such as Speed Kings, Battle Kings, Sky Kings, etc. The first runs of these larger models were in quite garish colours, but they were not well received by the market, so more realistic paintwork was introduced. However, at that time, general economic factors were putting pressure on the company to make a decent profit. By the end of 1970, the company was running at a £700,000 loss due to the cost of re-tooling, and it had a £2m HMRC tax bill to pay from the heady days of enormous sales in the late 1960s. It had almost gone from riches to rags in just two years.

Around this time, too, Lesney sought the input of the growing collectors' market. They sent reps out to collectors' clubs and swap meets to see what their interests were, and from this was born several models for collectors and promotionals in the Yesteryear range. Whilst promotionals had featured in the company's repertoire since the 1960, in the 1970s this was a firmly established range of models, and it signalled a route of models aimed at collectors which proved to be very profitable.

It is reported that Jack Odell mentioned around this time that the company was 'arguing whether we could afford to buy a new typewriter'. It is imagined therefore that things were becoming fraught and finances tight at Lesney HQ, when just a few months before they had been awash with money. It must have taken expert persuasion for the banks to agree to extend credit, but they did, thanks to Jack's persistence.

The recovery plan involved closing of factories, and staffing was reduced by about 900 people, but now the company was able to diversify and spread the risk a bit. They did this by acquisitions and introducing new lines. They produced Matchbox Kits to rival Airfix, they bought Surtees Formula 2 sponsorship, they acquired Vogue Dolls from Tonka, and they made their own Disco Dolls. In the mid-late 1970s, they introduced plastic games such as Cascade and action figures such as Fighting Furies. But things didn't improve immediately, and 1973 in particular was a very tough year for Lesney as Jack Odell resigned as director. He had spent decades at the helm, steering the start-up company onwards and upwards to become a multi-award winning, stellar achieving global concern. But he now wanted out to spend time on his golf and enjoy many more holidays overseas.

At the beginning of 1974, there was general discontent in the industrial workplace in the UK. In February, coal miners launched industrial action which continued for eight weeks and meant power cuts to non-essential businesses like Lesney. Although the company's own industrial relations had been good, relative to the industry, the strike by the Fettling Department caused disruption. But by far the biggest problem was caused by the fire and flood at the Rochford factory, which resulted in the waste of millions of plastic parts for cars and which put the tooling out of action. Lucrative Yesteryear production was suspended for two years, and the newly repaired factory had to switch to other lines. However, this switch to other lines and the strategy taken by the board to pare down the workforce worked, as sales rose from £32.5m in 1975 to £88.9m in 1977, and in 1978 profits returned as the company made £5.4m –

this was a massive achievement to turn around a £700,000 loss in 1970 to such a strong profit. The workforce was back up to 6,000, the company won its fifth Queen's Award for Industry, and it still held a mighty 1.5m sq ft of manufacturing floor space, all of which was in and around north and east London and Essex.

However, some acquisitions did not work. Acquiring AMT Kits in the US in late 1978 was an expensive affair, as it cost £4.8m to buy. Lesney borrowed heavily in order to purchase it, and at very high interest rates. In 1978/79, Sterling was strong against the Dollar, which made for high prices in the export market, and with US exports making up a large proportion of Lesney's sales, they were in trouble once again. The predicted profits of £9.9m in 1978 were not achieved, and the balance sheet came in at £6.8m. In addition, those manufacturers who had made redundancies and switched toy production from the UK to Hong Kong were enjoying tariff-free sales in the US. But Lesney, who had kept manufacturing at home, were paying 12% on everything they exported. Mattel had been canny and had realised in 1968/9 that manufacturing in the Far East was key to keeping costs down and margins high, so they switched to Hong Kong very early on in the history of Hot Wheels. However, the directors at Lesney had never wanted this, preferring instead to keep jobs in the UK, and it wasn't until 1980 that Universal Toys persuaded them to switch some manufacturing to the Far East. But for now, things were looking decidedly grim once again.

By the end of the 1970s, Britain was at the beginning of a recession and all manufacturers were struggling to survive. The mighty manufacturers of Dinky and Corgi ceased trading in 1981 after decades of successful toy sales, and this would have been a very worrying signal for Lesney. Seeing the predicament his beloved former business was in, Jack came out of retirement in 1981 to help Lesney. At an emergency board meeting, the decision was made to borrow heavily from the bank in order to keep the company afloat.

But the loan from the bank didn't succeed in keeping the business running. In April 1982, the company reported operating losses of £84m and, under pressure from creditors, a buyer was urgently sought for the business. Try as they might, the directors could not find a purchaser for the business in such a depressed UK manufacturing market, so with the absence of a buyer on the horizon and with massive debt repayments to make, the death knell of Lesney Products & Company

Limited was ringing in everybody's ears.

Sadly, on June 11th, 1982, the business was declared bankrupt and subsequently closed. Receivers were appointed, and many thousands of people lost their jobs. After 35 years Lesney was finished.

It was reformed as Matchbox Toys Ltd. and assets were disposed of (Jack Odell bought some of the tooling and machinery which he used for Lledo Toys).

Both Mattel and Fisher Price were in the fray as buyers, but ultimately it was Universal Toys who would become the successor of the brand, which they bought on September 24th, 1982 for, reportedly, a knock-down price.

> **Mattel bought out the Matchbox brand in 1997 for a reported $755m with a workforce of 26,000 employees worldwide**

The tooling for the Matchbox range was slowly moved to Macau and in May 1983 the first Macau Matchbox toy was produced, thus ending the manufacture of Matchbox toys in the UK forever.

No.73a Leyland Pressure Refueller

No.74a Mobile Refreshments Canteen

No.75a Ford Thunderbird

No.75a Ford Thunderbird

124

GUIDE NOTES

PRICE GUIDE

PRICES FOR MATCHBOX TOYS have increased markedly during 2020-2022. This price guide is based on actual sales figures achieved by Maseytoys during 2021 and 2022. We have taken an average price achieved for each model, depending on condition (mint, good, etc). With rarer items, we have used recent sales figures which these have achieved at auction.

CONDITION

We have used the traditional guides of mint, excellent, very good, good, fair and playworn.

MINT – as it left the factory, including any factory flaws, in mint box.

EXCELLENT – with one or two tiny 0.5mm nibbles (not chips) in a complete, excellent box, no crushing or creasing, few corner scuffs, showing little sign of use.

VERY GOOD – with a few tiny 0.5mm nibbles, some rub to high points in a complete very good box, with slight crushing or creasing and some corner rub, showing few signs of use.

GOOD – some chips (1mm) and nibbles (0.5mm) and high point rub in a good complete box, with slight crushing and slight creasing, corner rub, showing some signs of use.

FAIR – overall chips, nibbles, and high point rub in a fair box, with one or two flaps missing, crushing and creasing, showing signs of much use.

PLAYWORN – much paint loss, all surfaces affected, parts missing in a playworn box with flaps missing, creasing, crushing, and in a very worn condition.

BOXED OR UNBOXED? - The values shown are for mint toys in mint boxes. This means that both the model and the box should be exactly as they left the factory. If your model is anything less than this, then reduce the value shown by the percentage given (this is a guide only):

Excellent boxed – reduce value by 40%
Very good boxed – reduce value by 50%
Good boxed – reduce value by 65%
Fair/playworn boxed – reduce value by 80%

Mint unboxed – reduce value by 50%
Excellent unboxed – reduce by 65%
Very good unboxed – reduce value by 70%
Good unboxed – reduce value by 75%

MASEYTOYS

MATCHBOX PRICE GUIDE

BPW/R/T - black plastic wheels/rollers/tyres
GPW/R/ - grey plastic wheels/rollers/tyres
SPW/R - silver plastic wheels/rollers
UDW/R - unpainted diecast wheels/rollers
K - knobbly tread
S - smooth tread

1a Aveling Barford Road Roller

Roof 1 (deep arch) £190.
Roof 2 (shallow arch) c.£850.
Roof 3 (straight) £80.
Yellowish green £175.
Pale green £220 by the percentage given (this is a guide only).

1b Aveling Barford Road Roller	57mm £60.
1c Aveling Barford Road Roller	57mm green driver £35.
1d Aveling Barford Road Roller	67mm £22.
1e Mercedes Covered Truck	£22.
2a Muir Hill Site Dumper	Unpainted diecast wheels £40. Green diecast wheels £82.
2a Muir Hill Site Dumper	Unpainted diecast wheels £35. GPW £35.
2c Muir Hill Site Dumper	Red body, green bucket, Laing £27. Red body, green bucket, Muir Hill £85. Green body, red bucket £2,000+ (estimate).

2d Mercedes Covered Trailer

£19

3a Cement Mixer

Blue with orange diecast wheels £45.
Blue with grey plastic wheels £60.
Green with orange diecast wheels £1500+ (estimate).

3b Tipper Truck

Grey cab, red or maroon tipper, BPW £55.
Red tipper with 11.5 x 45, GPW £230.
Maroon tipper with 11.5 x 45, GPW £300.

3c Mercedes Ambulance

Cream or white with red cross decal or label £27.
With enlarged wheel arch openings £95.

4a Massey Harris Tractor

Red body, tan farmer, crimped axles, UDW £40.

4c Triumph Motorcycle & Sidecar

Steel blue with 4 on base £65.
With 78 on base £400 (estimate).
Metallic copper with 4 on base £2000+ (estimate).

4d Dodge Stake Truck

Green plastic stake back £26.
Blue plastic stake back £55.

5a London Double Decker Bus

Red body £50.
Green body £6,000 (estimate).

5b London Double Decker Bus

Red body, BRIGHT yellow decals, UDW £50.
Duller yellow decals £40.
Player's decals, GPW £85.
BP decals, GPW £220.

5c London AEC Routemaster Bus

Red body, BP visco-static decals, BPW/GPW £30.
Red body, Player's decals, BPW/GPW £125.
Red body, Peardrax decals BPW/GPW £135.

5c London AEC Routemaster Bus (cont.)

Red body, Mecca/Baron of Beef decals (beware).

Red body, BP Longlife decals, BPW £45.
Red body, BP visco-static decals or labels, BPW £35.

5d London AEC Routemaster Bus

Red body, Baron of Beef decals, BPW £395.
Red body, Pegram labels, BPW £550.
Red body, News of the World decals, BPW £500+ (estimate).

6a Quarry Truck

Orange cab, grey tipper, UDW £40.
GPW £4000+ (estimate).

6b Euclid 4 Wheel Quarry Truck

Yellow body, BPW rounded axle ends £45.
Crimped axle ends £65.
GPW £3000+ (estimate).

6c Euclid 6 Wheel Quarry Truck

Yellow with black hydro-sleeve £35.
White hydro-sleeve £185.

6d Ford Pick Up Truck   Red body, BPW £32.

7a Horsedrawn Milk Float   Orange with white crates and driver, UDW £85.
                                    Orange with white crates and driver, GPW £120.
                                    Silver crates and driver £700+ (estimate).

7b Ford Anglia   Blue body, SPW/BPW £40.
                                    GPW £55

7c Ford Refuse Truck   Orange cab, silver/grey back £25.

8a Caterpillar   Yellow body with yellow driver £38.
                                    Orange £125.
                                    Yellow body with red driver £250-350.

8b Caterpillar   42mm long yellow body and driver £45.

8c Caterpillar   48mm long UDR £35.
                                    BPR £40.
                                    SPR £70.

8d Caterpillar	Yellow, without driver £35.
8e Ford Mustang	White body £35. Red/orange body £390.
9a Dennis Fire Engine	Red body, gold trim, no details to grille, UDW £40.
9b Dennis Fire Engine	Red body, gold trim, detailed grille, UDW £50. GPW £300+ (estimate).
9c Merryweather Fire Engine	Red body, gold ladder, rounded axle ends, BPW £45. Red body, tan ladder, rounded axle ends, BPW £60. Red body, silver ladder, rounded axle ends, BPW £67. GPW, rounded axle ends £47. GPW, crimped axle ends £57.

9d Cabin Cruiser Boat & Trailer

Blue Deck £25.
Matt turquoise deck £30+ (estimate).

10a Scammell Mechanical Horse

Red cab, gold trim, grey trailer, 56mm £47.

10b Scammell Mechanical Horse

Red cab, gold trim, tan trailer larger size £47.
GPW £75.

10c Foden Sugar Truck

Blue body, Tate & Lyle decals, BPW £45.
SPW £75.
GPW £50.
GPW with crown on rear decal £75.

10d Leyland Pipe Truck

Red body, chrome grille £25.
White grille £55.

11a ERF Petrol Tanker

Red body, UDW £60.
Yellow body £70.
Green body £1000+ (estimate).

11b ERF Petrol Tanker

Red body, Esso decal, UDW, silver trim £65.
GPW £50.
BPW £120.
UDW, gold trim £220.
SPW £2000+ (estimate).

11c Jumbo Mobile Crane

Yellow body, BPW £25.
12x45, BPW £95.

11d Mercedes Scaffold Truck

Silver body, scaffolds & planks £25.

12a Land Rover

Green or blue body, tan luggage, BPW £45.
Gold body, BPW £2000+ (beware copies).
Silver boy, BPW £2000+ (beware copies).

13a Bedford Wreck Truck

Tan body, red jib £45.

13b Bedford Wreck Truck

Tan body, red jib, longer sides to back than 13a.
UDW £40.
GPW £85.

13c Ford Thames Trader Wreck Truck

Dark red body, closed or open jib lattice, unpainted or red hook:
BPW, outlined decals £45.
Non-outlined decals £55.
GPW, knobbly tread £65.
GPW, fine tread £85.

13d Dodge Wreck Truck

Yellow cab, green back, grey or red plastic hook, BP decal with white background £40.
BP decal without white background £155.
Green cab, yellow back thick booms, crimped axle ends, BP labels £2250.
Green cab, yellow back thin booms, rounded axle ends, BP decals £4000+ (estimate).

14a Daimler Ambulance

Cream body, silver trim, UDW £35.

14b Daimler Ambulance

Cream body, red cross decals, UDW £40.
GPW £80.
SPW £175.

14c Bedford Lomas Ambulance

Cream body, red cross roof decal, smooth roof, BPW £35.
SPW £155.
GPW £185.
With cross locating guides to roof, BPW £600.
SPW £250.
GPW £375.

14d Iso Grifo Coupe

Dark blue body, chrome hubbed wheels, blue interior £40.
Metallic blue £85.
White interior £300-400 (estimate).
With F type box (has model number on picture side at top right-hand corner) add £80

15a Diamond T Prime Mover

Orange, UDW £50.
Yellow, UDW £800-£1000.
Orange, GPW £300-£500.

15b Rotinoff Prime Mover

Orange body, BPW £45.
GPW, rounded axle ends £800-1000.
GPW, crimped axle ends £2000-£3000.

15c Dennis Refuse Truck

Blue cab, grey tipper, cleansing decals, with vent hole to tipper unit £40.
10x24, BPW £90.
10x24, BPW without vent hole £80.
11x 45, BPW, without vent hole £200-£300.

15d Volkswagen 1500 Beetle Saloon

White or cream body, black tyres, 137 decals £55.

16a Atlantic Trailer

Tan body, UDW £35.

16b Atlantic Trailer

Orange body, BPW £50.
Tan body, GPW £80.
Orange body, GPW £900-£1200.

16c Scammell Snowplough

Grey body, orange tipper, BPW £35.

16d Case Bulldozer

Red body, yellow blade £18.

17a Bedford Removal Van

Green body, UDW, removals decals £60.
Blue body £135.
Maroon body gold trim £120.
Maroon body, silver trim £190.

17b Bedford Removal Van

Bree body, flat roof, silver trim, removals decals, UDW £80.
GPW £125.
Dark green, GPW £190.

17c Austin Taxi	Maroon, grey interior, tan driver, GPW £65. SPW, light grey interior £125. SPW, darker grey interior £155.
17d Foden Hoveringham Tipper	Red cab, orange tipper, Hoveringham decals, BPW £35.
17e AEC Horsebox	Red body, green plastic horsebox £25.
18a Bulldozer	Yellow body and driver, red blade £45.
18b Bulldozer	Yellow body and driver, yellow blade £45.
18c Bulldozer	Yellow body, driver and blade, 58mm, BPR £30. UDR £30. SPR £100.
18d Bulldozer	Yellow body, no driver, yellow blade, BPR £35. SPR £70.

18e IHC Scout Field Car

Yellow body, red hubs, silver base £35,.
Black base £45.
Green hubs £150-250.

19a MG Midget Sports Car

Cream body £60.
White body £80.

19b MGA Sports Car

White body, UDW, silver trim £70.
GPW, silver trim £55.
SPW, silver trim £250.
UDW, gold trim £350.

19c Aston Martin DBR-5 Racing Car

Green body, 19 decal £85.
52 decal £220.
4,5 or 41 decal £300-500.

19d Lotus Racing Car

Green body £30.
Orange body £65.
19 or 5 decals £150-250.

20a ERF Stake truck

Maroon/dark red, UDW £60.
GPW £250.
Gold trim, UDW £250.
Green £2000+.

20b ERF686 Ever Ready Truck

Blue body BPW £70.
GPW £100.
SPW £200.

Orange body, ivory interior, plated base, BPW £40.
Orange body, red interior, plated base, BPW £60.
Orange body, ivory interior, silver painted base, BPW £80.
Orange body, GPW £2500+.
Yellow body, red interior, plated base, BPW £40.
Yellow body, ivory interior, plated base, BPW £120.

20c Chevrolet Taxi

21a Bedford Coach

Green, UDW, silver trim £65.
Gold trim £150.

21b Bedford Coach

Green, UDW, silver trim, 58mm £85.
GPW £110.
Dark green, GPW £135.
Dark green, SPW £5000+.

21c Commer Milk Float

Green body, BPW £40.
SPW, cow decal, green glazing £50.
SPW, bottle decal £45.
Clear windows £150.
GPW £200.
Light blue body £300+.

21d Foden Cement Mixer

Yellow cab, red body, BPW £25 .

22a Vauxhall E Series Cresta 1956

Maroon/dark red body, UDW £45.

22b Vauxhall PA Series Cresta 1958

Light or dark metallic copper £160.
Light or dark metallic gold £160.
Grey & lilac £150.
Metallic brown and sea green £190.

22b Vauxhall PA Series Cresta 1958 (cont.)

Cream £100.
Pink £150.
Pink UDW £1000+.
Pink & sea green £3200.

22c Pontiac Grand Prix

Red body BPW £50.
Orange body £80.

23a Berkley Cavalier Caravan

Pale blue, UDW £40.

23b Berkley Cavalier Caravan

Pale blue, UDW £40.
Lime green, UDW £60.
Lime green, GPW £50.
Metallic lime green £1000.

23c Bluebird Dauphine Caravan

Metallic mauve, GPW or SPW £50.
BPW £250.
Crimson base, black door, GPW £1000.
SPW, green glazing £1000.
Metallic lime green £650.

23d Trailer Caravan

Yellow or pink body, BPW £35.
Yellow, GPW £1850.

24a Weatherill Excavator Yellow, UDW £25.
Orange, UDW £35.

24b Weatherill Excavator Yellow-orange, BPW, 68mm £25.
GPW, rounded axle ends £30.
GPW crimped axle ends £80.

24c Rolls Royce Silver Shadow Metallic red body £30.

25a Bedford Dunlop Van Blue body, Dunlop decals, UDW £40.
GPW £60.
BPW £2000+.

25b Volkswagen Beetle Metallic steel blue body, glazing, either correct or incorrect spelling of Volkswagen, GPW £100.
SPW £160.
BPW £2000+.

25c Bedford BP Petrol Tanker Green, yellow and white with BP decals, GPW £45.
BPW £1300.

25c Bedford BP Petrol Tanker (cont.)

Blue and white with ARAL decals £280.
Green, yellow and white with ARAL decals £350.

25d Ford Cortina MkII

Metallic brown body, BPW £30.
Gift set G4 model with yellow roof rack £70.

26a ERF Cement Mixer

Orange with silver trim, UDW £55.
GPW £85.
SPW £550.
Gold trim, UDW £380.

26b Foden Cement Mixer

Orange body, orange barrel, BPW £40.
GPW £60.
Grey barrel, GPW £1200.
Orange barrel, SPW £2000+.

26c GMC Tipper

Red cab, silver tipper, green chassis, BPW £25.

27a Bedford Low Loader	Green cab, tan trailer, UDW £80. Blue cab, tan trailer, £190. Blue cab, dark blue trailer, £900.
27b Bedford Low Loader	Light green cab, tan trailer, UDW £100. GPW £200. Dark green cab £250.
27c Cadillac Sixty Special	Metallic lilac body, black base, GPW £80. SPW £110. BPW £150. Crimson base, SPW/GPW £100. Silver grey body £100. Metallic green body £320. Metallic mauve body £200.
27d Mercedes 230sl Convertible	White body, red interior, BPW £40.
28a Bedford Compressor Truck	Matt or gloss orange body, UDW £50. Yellow body £60.

28b Thames Trader Compressor Truck

Yellow body, silver trim, 10mm x 24 tread, BPW £50.
All other BPW £80.
GPW £2800+.

28c Jaguar Mk10

Metallic brown, BPW £25.
BPW, four-line base 9mm x 36 tread, BPW £80.
BPW, three-line base £1000+.
GPW, three-line base £4000+.

28d Mack Dumper Truck

Orange body, red or yellow plastic wheels £25.

29a Bedford Milk Float

Tan body, white load, UDW £40.
GPW £60.

29b Austin A55 Cambridge

Two-tone green body, BPW £50.
SPW £60.
GPW £75.

29c Fire Pumper

Red body, white accessories, BPW £25.

30a Ford Prefect

Brown/fawn body, UDW £45.
GPW £80.
Pale green body, UDW £90.
Blue body, GPW £260.

30b Magiruz Deutz 6-Wheeled Crane

Silver body, orange jib, BPW £45.
SPW £90.
GPW £100.
Brown body red or orange jib, £6800 (sold at auction 2014).

30c Faun 8-Wheeled Crane

Green body with rear brace £40.
Without brace £60.
Turquoise body sold in 2008 for £2800.

31a Ford Customline Stationwagon

Yellow body, UDW £80.
GPW £80.

31b Ford Fairlane Stationwagon

Green body, pink roof, crimson base, SPW £90.
GPW £100.
Black base, GPW £100.
BPW/SPW £120.
Yellow body, crimson base, SPW, glazing £300.
Without glazing £450.
Yellow body, black base £1200.

31c Lincoln Continental

Turquoise body, BPW £50.
Metallic dark blue £60.
Metallic lime green sold at auction in 2017 £2500.

32a Jaguar XK140

White body, UDW £70.
GPW £80.
Red body, GPW £120.
Orange-red body, GPW £140

32b Jaguar E-type

Metallic red BPT £60.
GPT, clear glazing £80.
GPT, green tinted glazing £160.
Metallic bronze, GPT £500+.

32c Leyland Petrol Tanker

White and green body, BP decals or labels, chromed grille £40.
White grille £60.
Blue and white, ARAL labels £180.

33a Ford Zodiac MkII

Dark green, UDW £80.
Sea Green Body, any wheels £90.
Flat dark green, UDW £250.
Metallic mauve and orange body, SPW, glazing £100.
UDW/GPW £150.
GPW green windows £200-300.
GPW without windows £160.
Teal blue, UDW £400-500.
Light blue body, UDW/GPW £170.
Dark blue body, UDW sold at auction in 2008 £850.

33b Ford Zephyr 6 MkIII

Turquoise body BPW £30.
SPW £50.
GPW £50.
Light Sea Green £85.

All have chrome hubbed wheels.
Yellow body, red interior, clear engine glazing £50.
Frosted engine glazing £100.
Ivory interior £750.
Gold body, cream interior £320.
Gold body, red interior £500+.

33c Lamborghini Miura

34a Volkswagen Van

Green body knobbly tread, GPW £70.
Fine tread, GPW £100.
KBPW £100.
FBPW £560.
SPW sold January 2021 £2000.

34b Volkswagen Camper

Green body knobbly tread, GPW £70.
Fine tread, GPW £100.
KBPW £100.
FBPW £560.
SPW sold January 2021 £2000 .

34c Volkswagen Camper

Silver body BPW low roof £45.
High roof £100.
With F-type box add £20.

35a ERF Horsebox

Red cab, tan body, UDW £45
GPW £75.
BPW £100.
SPW £150.

35b Snow Trac

Red body BPR, white rubber tracks £40.

36a Austin A50 Cambridge

Various shades of blue-green, UDW £35.
GPW £60.
Pale blue, GPW £75

36b Lambretta Scooter & Sidecar

Light metallic green, BPW £100.
Dark metallic green £80.

Gold body, black diecast base, BPW, chromed engine £40.

36c Opel Diplomat

Grey engine £60.
Turquoise-light blue body, plastic base sold in 2020 £11,000.

37a Karrier Bantam Coca-Cola Truck

Yellow body UDW, even load £60.
Even load, GPW £80.
Uneven load £125.

37b Karrier Bantam Coca-Cola Truck

Yellow body, with basplate, UDW £65.
GPW £75.
BPW £90.
SDW £900.

37c Dodge Cattle Truck

Orange-yellow cab, grey plastic back, with braces below cattle box £45.
Without braces £110.

38a Karrier Refuse Truck

Grey body, UDW £35
GPW £100.
Silver body, GPW £50.
SPW £500+.
Grey-brown body £100.

38b Vauxhall Victor Estate

Yellow body, red interior, GPW £55.
Green interior, BPW £45.
GPW £50.
SPW £60.

38c Honda Motorcycle & Trailer

Yellow trailer with BPW, metallic green Honda, £45
Orange trailer without decal £60.
Orange trailer with decal £180.

39a Ford Zodiac Convertible

Peach body, sea green base, UDW £65.
GPW £90.
Light green base, UDW, closed side quarterlight windows £50.
Open quarterlights £250.
GPW £50.

39a Ford Zodiac Convertible (cont.)

Blue base, GPW £90.
SPW £140.
Tan base, UDW, closed side quarterlight windows £120.
Tan, open quarterlights £380.

39b Pontiac Convertible

Yellow, black base, any type wheels £80.
Maroon base, SPW/GPW £60.
Metallic violet, maroon base, SPW £140.
GPW £700+.

39c Ford Tractor

Blue Body £25.
Blue and yellow body, short 5mm exhaust £25.
Long 7mm exhaust £120.
Orange body £60.

40a Bedford S-Type Tipper

Red body, tan tipper, UDW £40.
GPW £50.

40b Leyland Coach | Light metallic blue body, BPW/SPW £40.
GPW £85.

40c Farm Trailer | Blue body, yellow hubs £20.

41a Jaguar D-type | Green body, UDW, 41 decal £60.
52 decal £520.
GPW, 41 decal £100.

41b Jaguar D-Type | Green Body, GPW, 41 decals open grille £55.
Closed grille, 41 decals £80.
Spoked wheels, 41 decals £80.
5 decals £190.
Red 6 decals sold in 2008 £1300.
Red plastic hubs, closed grille, 41 decals £300.

41c Ford GT 40 | White body, yellow hubs £35.
Red hubs £380.
Spoked wheels £200+.

41c Ford GT 40 (cont.)

Cream body, yellow hubs £1500+.
Yellow body, yellow hubs £290.

42a Bedford Evening News Van

Orange-yellow body, UDW/KGPW £70.
KBPW £80.
FGPW/FBPW £175.

42b Studebaker Lark Station Wagon

Light blue body, light blue sliding roof, BPW £35.
Dark blue body, light slide £45.
Dark blue body, dark slide £70.

42c Iron Fairy Crane

Red body, yellow jib, one high, one low pin to jib £20.
Two high pins to jib sold 2020 £1800.

43a Hillman Minx

Blue-grey body, cream roof, UDW £50.
GPW £70.
Turquoise body, GPW £90.
Green body, UDW £320.

43b Aveling Barford Tractor Shovel

Yellow body & shovel, red driver & base £25.
Yellow body, driver & base, red shovel £40.
Yellow body, driver, base, shovel £150.
Yellow body, red driver, red base, red shovel £320.

43c Pony Trailer

Yellow body, green base £20.
With brown base £30.

44a Rolls Royce Silver Cloud

Metallic blue UDW £35.
GPW £60.
SPW £60.

44b Rolls Royce Phantom V

Metallic mauve BPW £50.
GPW £120.
SPW £290.
Silver grey, BPW £100.
SPW £290.

44c GMC Refrigerator Truck

Red cab, turquoise back, BPW £25.

45a Vauxhall Victor FA Series

Yellow body, UPW without glazing, with dashboard brace £45.
Without dashboard brace £300.
GPW, with clear glazing £75.
GPW, green glazing £50.
SPW, green glazing £60.
BPW, green glazing £80.
Red body, UPW £3600+.

45b Ford Corsair & Boat

Pale yellow body, red interior, BPW, unpainted base £40.
BPW, silver base £60.
GPW £80.
White interior, BPW unpainted base £3000+.

46a Morris Minor 1000

Green body, UDW £70.
Blue body, UDW £80.
Blue-green body, GPW £100.
Blue body, GPW £100.
Tan body UDW £3000+.

46b Guy Pickford's Removal Van

First casting with ridge to front and lined grille, blue body, 3-line decals, GPW £120.
With SPW £120.
Second casting with flat front and checkered grille, blue body, 3-line decal, GPW £50.
Blue, SPW £100.
Blue, 2-line decal, GPW £170.
Blue SPW £300.
Green body, 3-line decal, SPW or GPW £60.
BPW £140.
BPW with black rear bumper £120.
With 2-line decal, BPW £500+.
Tan body, Beales promotional £800.

46c Mercedes Benz 300SE

Green body, BPW £40.
Blue body, BPW £40.
With F-type box £60.

47a Trojan Brooke Bond Van

Dark red body, UDW £60.
GPW, crimped axle ends, silver grille £80.
D-Type box, GPW £450.

47b Commer Ice Cream Van

Blue body, BPW £60.
GPW £300.
Metallic blue body BPW £90.
Cream body, striped decals, BPW £320.
Oval decals £60.

47c DAF Container Truck

Silver body, BPW £25.
Turquoise body BPW £50.

48a Meteor Sports Boat & Trailer

Blue hull, tan deck, black trailer, UDW £50.
GPW £80.
SPW £120.

48b Sports Boat & Trailer

Red and cream or red and white plastic boat, blue trailer, BPW £60.
GPW £130.

48c Dodge Dump Truck

Red body, chromed plastic base, BPW £25.

49a M3 Halftrack

Military green body, GPW/UDW with UDR £35.
BPW with small BPR £50.
BPW with large BPR £70.
GPW with SPR £120.
GPW with GPR £250.

49b Mercedes Unimog

Tan body, turquoise base, orange plastic hubs £30.
Turquoise body red base £30.
With F-type box £40.
Tan body, red base £1000+.

50a Commer Mk VIII Pick-up

Tan body, UDW or GPW £50.
Darker tan, SPW £120.
Red and grey body, BPW £150.
Red and grey, SPW or GPW £100.
Red and white body, SPW or GPW £1800.

50b John Deere Tractor

Green body, orange/yellow plastic wheels, black tyres £30.
Grey tyres £40.
Green body, red or green plastic hubs £2000+ (redhubs sold in 2006 £4000).

50c Ford Kennel Truck

Metallic green body, silver grille, textured loadbed £50.
With white grille, textured loadbed £50.
White grille with smooth loadbed £60.

51a Albion Chieftain Portland Cement Truck

Yellow body, tan load, UDW, Portland or Blue Circle decal £50.
With GPW £100.
Large SPW £160.
Small SPW £320.
Small BPW £220.

51b John Deere Trailer

Green body, yellow hubs, yellow barrels, BPW £25. GPW £35.
With green or red hubs £300+.
Blue with yellow hubs £500+.
With orange barrels £200+.

51c AEC 8-Wheel Tipper

Orange body, Douglas labels, silver grille £60.
With white grille £90.
With Pointer labels £180.
Yellow body, Douglas labels £60.
With Pointer labels £40.
Alcan promotional £300+.

52a Maserati 4CLT Racer

Red body, BPW, without decal £60.
With 52 decal £70.
With spoked wheels £250.
Yellow body, spoked wheels, '52' decals £100.
With '5' decals £200.
With '3' decals £360.
With '41' decals £500+.

52b BRM Racer

Blue body, yellow hubs, 5 decal £30.
With 3 decal £90.
Red body £120.
Dark red body £200+.

53a Aston Martin DB 2-4 MkI

Metallic green body, UDW £80.
With GPW £120.
Metallic red body, BPW £180-220.
With GPW £260-360.
Flat red body, BPW £500+.
Silver body, UDW £2000+

53b Mercedes Benz 220 SE

Maroon body, SPW £60.
GPW £80.
BPW £120.
Dark red body, BPW £40.
GPW £120.
Metallic light blue body, BPW, cream interior £30.
With chromed hubs and tyres £500+.
With violet-lilac interior £1400.

53b Mercedes Benz 220 SE (cont.)

Metallic green body, sold for £3200 in 2013

53c Ford Zodiac Mk IV

Metallic light blue body, BPW, cream interior £30.
With chromed hubs and tyres £500+.
With violet-lilac interior £1400.
Metallic green body, sold for £3200 in 2013.

54a Saracen Personnel Carrier

Military green with BPW, closed rear base £40.
With open rear base £100.

54b S&S Ambulance

White body, BPW, small labels or decals £30.
Large labels £60.

55a DUKW Amphibian Truck

Military green, UDW £35.
With GPW £45.
With BPW £55.

55b Ford Fairlane Police Car

Metallic blue body.
BPW £80.
SPW £600.

55b Ford Fairlane Police Car (cont.)	GPW £500. Dark gloss blue body, BPW £260.
55c Ford Galaxy Police Car	White body, Police decals, BPW, red roof light £35. Blue light £400.
55d Mercury Police Car	White body, Police decals, BPW, red roof light £400+. Blue light £70.
56a Trolleybus Peardrax	Red body, Peardrax decals, red poles, UDW or GPW £65. BPW £75. SPW £200. Black poles £180. Visco decals £850+.
56b Fiat 500	Turquoise body, BPW, light or dark tan luggage £30. Red boy £100.
57a Wolseley 1500	Pale green, GPW, silver trim £40. Gold trim £260+.

57b Chevrolet Impala

Two-tone blue body, BPW £50.
GPW, black base £160.
GPW, blue base £200+.
SPW, dark blue base £80.
SPW, light blue base £200.
SPW, mid-blue base £240.
SPW, black base £65.

57c Land Rover Fire Engine

Red body, decals or labels, BPW £50.
With GPW £240.

58a AEC Coach BEA

Blue body, white decals, GPW £40;
BPW with red and black decals £120.
GPW £70.
SPW £500+.
Empty D-type box £950+.

58b Drott Excavator

Red body, UDR £150+.
BPR £100.
SPR £100.
Orange body, silver baseplate, BPR £70.
With SPW £150+.

58c DAF Girder Truck

White body, BPW, red girders £30.

59a Ford Thames Singer Van

Light green body, decal guides, Singer decals, GPW £110.
SPW £200;
Without decal guides £120.
Dark green, SPW £140.
GPW £180.

59b Ford Fairlane Fire Chief

Red body, Fire Chief decals, BPW £80.
GPW £190+.
SPW £250+, with shield decals £260+.

59c Ford Galaxy Fire Chief

Red body, BPW, blue light £50.
With red light, sold in 2009 for £950.

60a Morris J2 Pick-up

Blue body, red and white or red and black decals, BPW £50.
GPW £60.
SPW £80.

60b Leyland Site Truck Blue body, chromed plastic base, BPW £30.

61a Ferret Scout Car Military green, BPW £40.

61b Alvis Stalwart White body, BP decals, green plastic hubs, ribbed loadbed £40.
Smooth loadbed £60.
Yellow hubs, yellow canopy £70.
Yellow hubs, orange canopy £100+.
Military green £100.

62a AEC General Service Lorry Military green body, BPW, B-type box £40.
C-type box £70.
D-type box £90.

62b Commer TV Service Van Cream body Rentaset decals BPW £90.
Fine tread GPW £500.
Knobbly tread, GPW £500+.
Radio Rentals decals, BPW £80.
GPW £500+.

62c Mercury Cougar

Metallic green body, chrome wheels, wiper and mirror detail to windscreen £45.
Cream body, cream interior, without windscreen detail £4000+.
Cream body, red interior £3000.

63a Ford Service Ambulance

Military green body, red cross decal, BPW, B or C-type box £40.
D-type box £80.

63b Alvis Crash Tender

Red body, silver base, white plastic accessories, BPW £55.
12mm x 45 tread, BPW £100+.

63c Dodge Crane Truck

Yellow body, BPW £25.

64a Scammell Breakdown Truck

Military green body, BPW £55.

64b MG 1100

Green body, BPW £30

65a Jaguar 3.4 Litre Saloon

Gloss blue, blue numberplate GPW £40.
With silver numberplate £60.
Metallic blue £120.

65b Jaguar 3.8 Litre Saloon

Dark red body, BPW £130.
With GPW £40.
With SPW £50.
Metallic red body, SPW, clear gazing £90.
With green glazing £45.

65c Claas Combine Harvester

Red body, orange thresher and front hubs £20.

66a Citroen DS19

Yellow body GPW £80.
SPW £150.
With D-type box £700+.

66b Harley Davidson Motorcycle & Sidecar

Metallic bronze body, spoked wheels £80.

66c Greyhound Bus

Silver body, Greyhound labels or decals, BPW, amber glazing £30.
Clear glazing £80.

67a Saladin Armoured Car | Military green body, BPW, B, C or D-type box £40. E-type box £140.

67b Volkswagen 1600TL | Red body, chromed hub caps or wheels £35. Purple body with chromed caps or wheels £500+.

68a Austin Radio Truck | Military green body, BPW £45

68b Mercedes Setra Coach | Orange body, BPW £50. Turquoise body, BPW £130.

69a Commer Nestle Van | Maroon body, Nestle decals. KGPW £60. Red body, KGPW £70. FGPW £120. SPW £800+.

69b Hatra Tractor Shovel | Orange body, orange plastic wheels, grey tyres £70. Yellow body, red wheels £80.

69b Hatra Tractor Shovel (cont.)

Orange, yellow wheels, yellow shovel sold in 2008 £1900.
All others £25-35.

70a Ford Thames Estate Car

Yellow and turquoise body, GPW, SPW or BPW, rounded axle ends £40.
With crimped axle ends £60.

70b Ford Grit Spreader

Red body, lemon yellow hopper BPW £25.
Dark yellow hopper £35.

71a Austin 200 Gallon Tanker

Military green body, KBPW £60.
SBPW, D-type box £80.
Complete with button badge, add £20.

71b Jeep Gladiator Pick-up

Red body, white interior, BPW £45.
With green interior £65.

71c Ford Heavy Wreck Truck

Red cab and jib, white body, BPW, ESSO labels, green glazing £55. Amber glazing £350+.

72a Fordson Tractor

Blue body, GPW or BPW front wheels, orange or yellow rear wheels £45. All yellow wheels, GPT or BPT £400.
Yellow rear wheels, grey front wheels £500+.

72b Standard Jeep

Yellow body, yellow wheels, red interior £25. White interior sold in 2017 £1900.

73a Leyland Pressure Refueller

RAF blue body, GPW £80. BPW sold in 2009 for £2700.

73b Ferrari Racing Car

Red body, 73 decals, spoked wheels £55. With '52' decals £460.

73c Mercury Commuter

Metallic lime green body, cream interior, chromed wheels £25.

74a Mobile Refreshments Canteen

Silver body, dark blue base, GPW or SPW £90.
Sea green or sky-blue base £150+.
BPW sold in 2014 for £750.
Cream body, blue base, GPW £140.
Pale pink body £500+.
All others £40.

74b Daimler Fleetline Double Decker Bus

Red, green or cream body, ESSO labels, BPW in box with green bus illustration £35.
In box with red bus illustration £70.
Promotional labels £160+.

75a Ford Thunderbird

White and peach body, SPW, dark blue base £60.
GPW, dark blue base £110.
GPW, Mid-blue base £150.
GPW, Blue-green base,

75a Ford Thunderbird (cont.)

SPW £160.
Black base, SPW or GPW £140.
With blue-green base £400+.
Black base, BPW £160.

75b Ferrari Berlinetta

Metallic dark green body, spoked wheels £40.
With wheel hubs £50.
Metallic green, grey or silver base, spoked wheels £90.
Metallic green, unpainted base, spoked or hubbed wheels £40.
Metallic blue-green body £130.
Red body, wheels hubs, cowled lights £400+.
Red body, wire wheels now cowl to lights £1000+.
Metallic gold body sold in 2014 for £2000.

ABOUT THE AUTHOR

NEIL MASEY has been a collector, writer, and dealer in Matchbox toys since the 1970s. He has written extensively on the subject for diecast magazines in the UK, and he has contributed to a number of Matchbox price guides. Through his company Maseytoys, he has sold over 100,000 Matchbox models since it was established in 2001. He lives in Sussex, England, with his lifelong partner and his much adored cats. Aside from Matchbox, he has many other interests, including a passion for singing gospel, and he has sung lead tenor in many gospel and soul choirs. He supports a number of homelessness, asylum, and BME charities via his cosmetics and beauty business, Mr Masey's Emporium.

184

www.ingramcontent.com/pod-product-compliance
Lightning Source LLC
Chambersburg PA
CBHW040932240426
43673CB00052B/1962